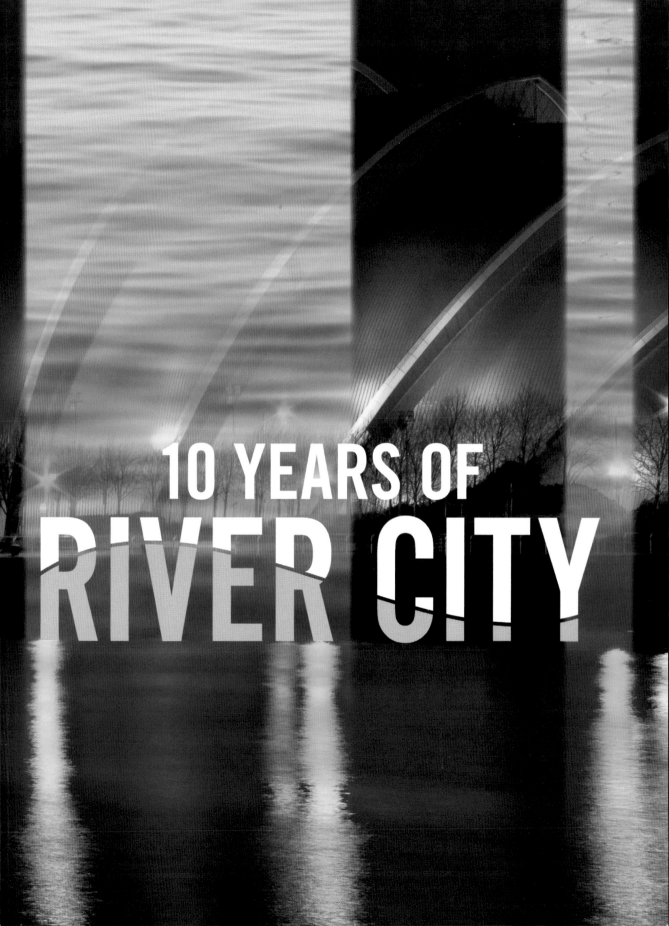

10 YEARS OF
RIVER CITY

BEHIND THE SCENES OF SCOTLAND'S FAVOURITE TV DRAMA

JEFF HOLMES

BLACK & WHITE PUBLISHING

First published 2012
by Black & White Publishing Ltd
29 Ocean Drive, Edinburgh EH6 6JL

1 3 5 7 9 10 8 6 4 2   12 13 14 15

ISBN: 978 1 84502 452 9

Copyright © Jeff Holmes 2012

Designed by Richard Budd Design
Printed and bound in Poland
www.hussarbooks.pl

CONTENTS

FOREWORD

By Johnny Beattie

Ten weeks can be a long time in showbiz but ten years – well, that's an eternity. I can't believe I've been part of a marvellous show for a decade, but it's hats off to everyone involved in *River City* because they've earned that longevity.

I remember getting the initial call from my agent, Anne Coulter, who said the BBC were keen to see me regarding a new project. 'Now,' she added. So up I toddled to Queen Margaret Drive where I met a lovely young lady called Victoria Beattie – no relation, by the way. We talked, drank coffee and went our separate ways.

Next day, they wanted to see me again. 'For more coffee?' I asked.

Ida Schuster, who would eventually play my partner-in-crime, Lily, was also there and we read a few lines from a prepared script. Then we had a cup of coffee!

Next day, Anne called again. 'They want to see you.'

'But I can't drink any more coffee . . .'

I was offered the part and the rest, as they say, is history. It was a blessing in disguise because I absolutely love being part of the show.

The moment I walked out onto the backlot I was completely mesmerised. It was a work of art and confirmed my already long-held belief that scenic artists truly are the unsung heroes of our industry and can create anything you ask for.

Initially I was given Malcolm's character background, and I was to be a Fifer who had previously worked on the railways.

'Is that okay?' asked the lady.

'Why can't I be a Glaswegian who worked in the shipyards because that's who I am?'

She said, 'That's brilliant!'

I was introduced to my 'daughters', Gina and Eileen – Libby McArthur and Deirdre Davis – and we have shared some fantastic moments. And I'm now playing alongside Eileen McCallum, another wonderful actor and person.

Before *River City*, the public knew me best as a variety entertainer and pantomime Dame. On one occasion I bumped into a wee wifey in Glasgow and she said to me, 'Johnny, I enjoy *River City* but I've seen you a lot funnier.' I told her I wasn't supposed to be funny because it was a straight part I was playing. She said, 'Aye, but when you used to dress up as a wummin you were a scream.' I told her they wouldn't let me dress up as a wummin on the show. But lo and behold, at the end of that year scriptwriters included a pantomime and I was picked to play Dame Disturbia! I could just see that wee wifey saying to her friends, 'That Johnny Beattie told me they wouldn't let him dress up as a wummin, and now look at him!'

I reckon I would like Malcolm if I met him in Montego Street because he's a sort of patriarch for the Shieldinch community and always trying to do the right thing. Early on in the show I was told I would be keeping doos (pigeons), which I knew absolutely nothing about. But I had this doo handler by my side constantly and he kept me right. On one occasion, I was to release four doos and the first three did exactly as they were told. The fourth, however, decided it didn't want to go out to play and flew right back at me, just missing my head. What's that they say about never working with pets?

But my time on the show has been just perfect and I wouldn't have swapped it for the world. Ten years have come and gone, and who would have thought that?

I'm immensely proud of everyone who has played their part, however small, in keeping our great show up there in the ratings. From my point of view, it has been a pleasure.

I'm sorted in Shieldinch. I have my own dressing room – right next to the toilets and the canteen!

Here's to the next ten!

RIVER CITY — The Commission

In 2000, BBC Scotland executive Ken McQuarrie spotted a gaping hole in the television schedule and moved quickly to fill it with a new Scottish soap. *River City* was commissioned and would go on to become a national institution, pulling in a remarkable half-million regular viewers each week. The show has also made household names of its actors . . . but we're getting ahead of ourselves. Here, Ken explains the story behind the inception of our favourite show and documents the trials and tribulations of inaugurating such a massive project – one that has lasted ten years, and beyond!

RIVER CITY – THE COMMISSION

K en McQuarrie had been mulling over a Scottish soap long before the new millennium, but when BBC Director General Greg Dyke announced in 2000 that funds would be made available for the nations and regions, Ken made his move. He pitched the idea to Mr Dyke, and he liked what he heard. The funding was granted and the well-oiled BBC Scotland drama machine clicked into 'soap mode'. But this one had to be a little different from its couthy predecessors: a gritty, urban representation of a thriving inner-city community. It was also a once-in-a-lifetime opportunity to create a 'star factory', a breeding ground for young talent to prosper both in front of, and behind, the camera. It was a massive challenge but one that Ken, who was then BBC Scotland's Head of Programmes, and his team tackled with gusto.

Ken insisted that his first battle, to inaugurate the soap, was one of the toughest. 'You're asking an audience to make a regular appointment to view, fifty-two weeks of the year. That's quite a commitment.

'The world of your programme has to be credible and relevant to a very broad section of the population, yet it must also be specific and true to its setting, which in this case was Glasgow. It must look and feel like real life, while being dramatically heightened and hooky enough to draw people back week after week. That's a lot of elements pulling in different directions. Creating a new soap is also a massive investment in terms of cost, time and effort. Getting it wrong would have been an expensive mistake.'

A myriad of people were involved in bringing the soap together from the initial idea to what we now see on our screens. From property experts, contract specialists, script and production staff to, ultimately, a talented cast and crew. But each new idea is dependent on having a person, or persons, with the creative mind and drive to take the strands of an idea and put the bones of the show in front of the decision makers. That man was Stephen Greenhorn.

Ken said, 'Devising a soap is quite a feat and requires someone with great vision, imagination and the ability to bring so many different stories to life in a really compelling way. Stephen brought all that to the table – and more.'

Many potential locations across the central belt were explored and while Ken admitted that Leith, on the outskirts of Edinburgh, had been

Ken McQuarrie

a genuine candidate, the BBC's preferred option was always to base the show reasonably close to their new Pacific Quay hub.

And while no one at the BBC would confirm the initial or final budgets, the figure being bandied about at the show's inception, of £10 million, would appear to have been put to good use. Whatever the sums, Ken agreed.

He said, 'We think it was money well spent. *River City* brings a very important audience to BBC Scotland. Portrayal is key and therefore it's important that we're making programmes that are culturally representative and relevant to our viewers. The show is loved by its loyal audience, evidenced by the fact that it regularly out-performs other continuing dramas in Scotland in terms of audience appreciation measures.'

And in the case of set design, Ken reckons there are few better. 'The set is magnificent and so accurately represents a Glasgow tenement street. So much thought and detail went into the original design. It's great fun showing visitors around because they never fail to be impressed by the sheer scale and realism.'

Midway through the show's ten-year existence, a decision was taken to switch from two half-hour episodes per week to a single, one-hour show. It was a decision that caught viewers on the hop, but one which had little effect on *River City*'s impressive audience figures.

Ken said, 'The switch had massive implications for the show in terms of how we told the stories and how we physically produced the episodes. It was a huge challenge at first – especially because the format of *River City* was designed to tell stories over thirty minutes, which is a very different proposition to telling bigger "stories of the week" over an hour.

'So many hour-long precinct shows are medical or crime-based because they lend themselves brilliantly to the medical emergency/crime-of-the-week format. In comparison, *River City* is a really tough show to write because the stories are harder to come by. It's not ideal to have to change format while remaining on air, but as a result of other soaps becoming more frequent, it became difficult to find two individual half-hour slots that didn't clash. Rather than going up against them it seemed best to transmit an hour of *River City* on a different night entirely.'

In 2002, at the launch of the 'Scottish soap', Ken went on record as saying that the BBC were in it for the long haul, so the million-dollar question is: Was there ever a point when he thought he might have to go back on his word?

And in a word, or two, he said, 'Thankfully, no!'

'I think the show has stood the test of time and lasted a decade because it's distinctive – there's no other show like it on TV and I believe that has definitely contributed to its success and longevity.'

'The set is magnificent and so accurately represents a Glasgow tenement street. So much thought and detail went into the original design. It's great fun showing visitors around because they never fail to be impressed by the sheer scale and realism.'

CHAPTER 1

Let's Make a Soap

BBC Scotland pulled off a masterstroke when they enlisted the services of Stephen Greenhorn. His remit? Devise a soap set in contemporary, urban Scotland. He got down to work but was forced to make several key changes when a top-level decision forced him to change direction, mid-stream. But with one of Scotland's top set designers on board, construction of the 'best backlot in the United Kingdom' got underway, and *River City* edged a step closer to reality. And then we had that catchy theme tune: brainchild of an Inverness-based Academy Award-winning composer of the future!

LET'S MAKE A SOAP

Some may struggle to recall the big game, but Stephen Greenhorn remembers it well. It was Tuesday, 24 September 2002, and the final result was *River City*: 1, Manchester United: 0. Scotland's new soap went head-to-head with United's Champions League match against Bayer Leverkusen and almost 750,000 people tuned in to the opening episode. It was a spectacular home win for the residents of Shieldinch.

When BBC Scotland decided to create its own drama serial, pitches were invited from independent producers. But the Corporation decided to launch an in-house bid and turned to Stephen for his thoughts. The forty-eight-year-old West Lothian man had just created *Glasgow Kiss* and was in the building for a series of meetings on a BBC part-funded play.

Stephen Greenhorn

At one such get-together he was let in on the top-secret plans for the soap. 'Good luck,' he thought and moved on. But he wasn't getting off that easily and was eventually invited to form part of the in-house bid – with just one rule: it wasn't to be set in either Glasgow or Edinburgh.

Stephen said, 'As far as I was concerned, these were the only two choices for an urban soap, and I mean no disrespect to Aberdeen and Dundee.'

BBC Scotland felt Glasgow was over-exposed at the time but Stephen was of the mindset that a soap set in, say, Stirling, simply wouldn't work.

'I had been working on a story about the opening of the Scottish Parliament and was spending a lot of time in Leith. One night I was sitting outside a bar when it suddenly came to me. Leith was buzzing and had such a rich mix of social classes that would lend itself perfectly to soap.

'There was the new Malmaison Hotel and the Royal Yacht Britannia, but just fifty yards away you still had girls working the streets. Across the shore there were millionaire's flats. We were looking to create a microcosm of modern, urban Scotland and here we had it all in one little street.'

Stephen shared his Eureka moment with BBC Scotland. 'I think I've solved your problem. A show that's not Edinburgh or Glasgow, has a real sense of community and will incorporate all types of social classes.'

The BBC loved the idea, thought it worth pursuing, and asked Stephen to put his ideas down in a document of sorts. It was the summer of 2000 and the first episode was still some two years away. Stephen said, 'That "document" took me around six months to complete. It was, effectively, BBC Scotland's in-house bid. It was around fifty to sixty pages in length and I was thrilled to be told just before Christmas that it had been successful.'

Stephen's soap was to be set in Leith and called *The Shore*. That was, until he was summoned to another meeting and a BBC Scotland executive said, 'We love the concept . . . but . . . we would like to set it in Glasgow!'

Stephen was already some way down the road of producing storylines and characters, and the decision set him back. 'Glasgow tends to separate its social classes and therefore you would need an excuse to, say, build a wine bar in a working-class area. With Leith, none of these issues existed, but Glasgow it was and I set about "westernising" what was salvageable.

'I knew it would be a mammoth project but it's not every day someone asks you to create what will hopefully turn out to be a long-running television show. It was a massive undertaking but also an incredible opportunity.

'The first thing I had to do was discover exactly where in Glasgow it was supposed to be set. It wasn't Partick, Govan or anywhere on the south side.'

He settled on Whiteinch, which isn't a million miles away from Partick, and the geographical uncertainty that had initially clouded matters lifted somewhat. Despite the massive shift in geography, he was determined to hang in there, probably out of loyalty to the stories and characters he had been working on for six months. His original commission covered the first three episodes, although he planned to stick around a bit longer to contribute to what he hoped would become an accepted and established Scottish soap.

'Another reason for sticking with it was to try and establish a drama

BBC Scotland

Episode One

By

Stephen Greehorn

February 2002

The contents of this document are the property of the British Broadcasting Corporation, and will remain so. They should be treated as HIGHLY PRIVATE and CONFIDENTIAL
Please note that it is the addressee's responsibility to safeguard this script and to treat its contents with the utmost confidentiality.

There are no offers implied in sending of the script

Episode One script

factory. It was becoming increasingly difficult for Scottish actors, writers and crew to get a credit on their CV, so this "factory", which would produce more than fifty hours of drama a year, was vital to the industry north of the border. There are loads of people working in theatre who simply can't get an opportunity to make the transition to television.'

Stephen and the team started producing script outlines and character biographies. Meanwhile, an old whisky and vodka bottling plant in Dumbarton, once the largest of its kind in Europe, had been identified as the setting for the show. BBC Scotland set about creating Shieldinch from scratch, with purpose-built backlot, studio facility and office accommodation.

The previous working title *The Shore* was dropped and programme bosses searched for a simple but striking alternative. At a brainstorming session, Stephen suggested simply 'Shieldinch', but it was rejected. He recalls writing 'River City People' on the whiteboard, which was later shortened. The show now had a title, but it was kept under wraps and referred to merely as the 'Scottish soap'.

It was decided to have two main families, one intact and working class, and the other, a fractured family unit. Two sisters sharing a flat, a couple of grumpy OAPs and a dynamic entrepreneur made up the original cast list.

One character that made the initial leap from bit-part player to 'best boy' was Shellsuit Bob, who, Stephen admitted, was introduced to help 'make up time'. He explained, 'Initial timings were a bit out and we decided to introduce an extra element, but as we were working so far in advance, it had to be something or someone that wouldn't impact on future storylines.

'We needed a bit of Glasgow humour, a wee pal for Derek Henderson. Someone with a swagger and a great sense of fun. Shellsuit Bob was that character.

'One of my favourite lines arrived in episode three, when Bob was talking to Roisin in Lazy Ray's. She's flicking through a novel and he says to her, "Oh, you can read then!" It was fantastic, and the look she fired back . . .'

Apart from taking its toll on his health, Stephen looks back on his time in Shieldinch with fondness, although he admitted to being perplexed at the initial media reaction. 'It was predictable, to say the least. They put the show on a pedestal before it had even started, got everyone excited, and then slagged it off after just one episode. It was a bit like writing a film review based on the opening credits.

'It wasn't relevant that 750,000 people tuned in for the first episode because we always knew that wouldn't be anywhere near our core

audience. Lots of people were curious to see what all the hype was about.

'BBC Scotland had commissioned 104 episodes and we had storylines in place for three years. These were short-, mid- and long-term. We knew where these characters were going years down the line but still we were judged after thirty minutes.'

The bottom line, though, was that the BBC had always been in it for the long haul and both parties were confident they could ride the waves of scepticism. The Corporation had initially targeted soap fans: those who watched *Corrie* and *EastEnders* were invited over to watch *River City* as well.

As the big day edged closer and Stephen was spending more and more time away from set racing to prepare scripts for the first day of filming, late-night writing sessions were beginning to take their toll on his health, and while he vowed to see it through to its start date, he had long decided not to stick around as part of the soap's writing pool.

'It was so stressful that even after I'd been gone for months, I was

BBC Head of Drama, Barbara McKissack

still struggling to write. *River City* had drained me but had been such an important project in the first place that I stuck with it.

'It was my baby, but I soon became that estranged parent who watches from the window and says, "That's them off to school now!"'

'I'm glad I stepped back when I did. I may have been a wreck but I learned so much, which has stood me in good stead ever since. After the soap I was exec. producer on a programme called *Marchlands* and was able to see problems from both sides.

'But I remember heading down to Dumbarton one day with BBC Head of Drama Barbara McKissack and thinking, "This is massive" – like a shopping centre development. I suddenly became aware of the scale of *River City*, but now I can look back on ten years of the show and while I'm not a faithful viewer anymore, I try and catch up whenever I can.

'I'm so glad they've retained the sense of humour that we set out to achieve. It's the essence of the Glaswegian character and so important to the show.'

He added, 'The first time I set eyes on the backlot I got the "wow" factor. I had been so busy writing that I hadn't seen it for a while and when it was complete it just blew me away.

'I'm so proud of the part I played in making it all happen. Here's to the next ten!'

With the creation of the show in good hands, executives turned their attention to finding the ideal production designer: someone capable of literally building a community from scratch. That person was Pat Campbell.

Pat Campbell and crew

Pat came with an impressive portfolio, with film credits such as *Small Faces* on her CV, but nothing gave her more satisfaction than creating her very own small town – but one you won't find on any Ordnance Survey map.

Pat, who trained as an interior designer, created arguably the biggest and best backlot in the soap world, but revealed how the real sense of satisfaction came when she was let loose on a local cash and carry – and blew £1,000 on sweets for the Oyster Café!

'It was like all my Christmases had come at once,' laughed Pat, a 'product' of Glasgow School of Art. 'You've heard the saying about a kid being let loose in a sweet shop? Well, that was me.'

After staging exhibitions in the Hunterian Gallery in Glasgow's West End, Pat moved to the BBC where she designed backdrops for shows such as *All Creatures Great and Small* and *Mug's Game*.

She was initially approached about *River City* by Barbara McKissack, but a dozen years on, she insists that if she knew then what she does now, she might not have accepted the job. She said, 'It was a massive undertaking. Imagine the scale of creating an entire community. We started from scratch and had to find a suitable location which provided everything we needed in terms of space, proximity to the city and scope for expansion.

'We looked at places like Port Glasgow and Erskine but when the location department discovered the Dumbarton site, I knew we had struck gold. It had everything we needed.'

Pat and her art department colleagues, her 'Dumbarton Rocks', were handed the series 'bible', which had been produced by Stephen. 'This told us our requirements in terms of families, shops and the pub, all that kind of stuff, but that was all,' she said.

'At first, producers were keen to get away from the idea of a pub being the central meeting place. We spoke initially about a distillery being the area's focal point, but that didn't get too far.

Tenement date

'We initially designed a shape based around the tenements. We wanted secret, hidden areas, corners and closes where there would be hushed conversations, forbidden looks and plenty of scope for the dramatic action to unfold.

'There are tenements in Glasgow that are probably more elegant than ours but that wasn't what we wanted. They had to be traditional yet functional, with the hint of a waterside location, which we indicated through boat references and the ferry sign.

'There are elements of the set itself that are very distinctively Glaswegian. We took the area and gave it a date, as you can see by the "1890" sign etched above No. 5 Montego Street.

'Then we started to construct an entire history. Once upon a time, Shieldinch would have been used to unload cargo from foreign parts: there would have been an isolated waterside pub, and our inspiration for The Tall Ship was the Ferry Inn in Renfrew, which sits by the water.

'The Tall Ship would have been the watering hole for sailors and

NEWSAGENTS
TOBACCONIST
CONFECTIONERY

MALIQUE'S MINI MARKET
NEWSAGENTS & GROCERS

TRANSCARDS
TOILETRIES
FROZEN FOOD

LOTTERY
PAY POINT
OFF SALES

★

GREETING CARDS
POWER CARDS
BUS PASSES

★

FRESH FRUIT
SWEETIES
GINGER

- 42 -
K. MALIQUE
0141-616-6400

CIGGARETTES
SOFT DRINKS
BALLOONS

★

POSTAGE STAMPS
ICE-CREAM
CHILLED FOODS

★

DELIVERIES
TINNED GOODS
VIDEO'S

OPEN 7 DAYS

OPEN 7 DAYS

Your QUALITY local Newsagent & grocer

Y   loc   gent & Grocer

Original scale drawing of corner shop

The Tall Ship...pre-show

gradually a whole community would have built up around it, starting with the warehouses, the boatyard and two-storey buildings that had been burnt down in a fire and eventually replaced by tenements and shops.

'We gave Shieldinch a whole history of its own based around what has happened up and down Clydeside, where areas have developed according to the trades and industries that employ the people.

'We were all so close to the project that we really couldn't see the enormity of what was being constructed right before our eyes. We were out on that set trudging around in our wellies all day every day, month after month. The weather was a nuisance and it rained constantly.

'We anticipated wet months during winter but when spring came and water was still running down buildings, we wondered if it would ever stop. But it did and we completed the task.

'The best part for me was when we had some local people visiting the set and they said, "Oh, I didn't know there were tenements here" – that was the moment we knew we had done something right.'

Pat added, 'We were based in Scotland, which is a rarity for such a mammoth project, and it was strictly Monday to Friday, another rarity!

'We were told to build as much as possible, even derelict buildings that could be used in the future, while we had the money to play with.'

Pat said, 'We visited the *EastEnders* set on a couple of occasions and that taught me one thing: build the set to last! *EastEnders* wasn't constructed with maintenance in mind and was costing them a small fortune. We learned a valuable lesson there.

'Initially, we had the ground surveyed and put in the foundations, drainage and electricity. It was starting to get real. We had our deadline, and while another month would've been great, we had what we had and that was it. Of course, we made it and filming started on time.'

Building site

Pat has only ever been back to the set once, while working on another production based within the Dumbarton hub. 'I was keen to have a look at the backlot and wandered round for a nosey but didn't get much further than the security barrier before being challenged by a guard, who said, "Sorry, but you can't go round there."

'I was eventually allowed a peek and realised that it definitely wasn't my baby anymore. Many changes had already been made, but one remained the same: the Oyster Café – my favourite set. I just stood there for a few moments drinking it all in. It was a strange moment but also a nice moment.'

With set construction and scripts at an advanced stage, producers moved onto another part of the Shieldinch jigsaw that required attention and were lucky enough to discover a man who was most certainly in tune with success.

While the *River City* 'family' has looked on with pride as actors such as Gray O'Brien (*Coronation Street*) and Jayd Johnson (*The Field of Blood*) have left for pastures new and maintained a high profile, there is one man pivotal to the Shieldinch success story who seldom rates a mention. His contribution appears at the start of every episode, yet the name Lorne Balfe would no doubt draw a bemused reaction from most viewers. In fact, when you dash into the kitchen to make a pre-programme

cuppa, Lorne ensures you don't miss the start of your favourite show! He is the man behind the catchy *River City* theme tune, among a great many others. His credits include movies starring A-listers Johnny Depp, Michael Caine and Leonardo DiCaprio.

The Inverness-based composer was among a number of people who initially pitched for the *River City* signature tune and by the time he had finished, Lorne had offered up eighteen different pieces – and the BBC chose the last! Speaking about his initial experience of writing the music, he admitted, 'When the job came up, the brief was vague. They wanted inner-city Glasgow and urban. In the end I tried to cover all bases, from traditional Scottish to classical, and also rock. I was delighted to get the job.'

Lorne is the son of music mogul David Balfe, who enjoyed a long and successful career in popular music, penning the number one Daniel Boone hit 'Beautiful Sunday', as well as having a spell in post-punk combo The Teardrop Explodes ('Reward', 'Treason'). David initially tried to steer his son away from the perils of the music business but Lorne pressed ahead and before long had written more than 200 advertising jingles, selling everything from furniture to Scotland's other national drink, Irn Bru.

His career cranked up a notch when he penned the theme tunes for TV programmes *Most Haunted*, *Shoebox Zoo* and the *Jeremy Kyle Show*. Lorne, who suffered from dyslexia at school, was ambitious and wrote to award-winning composer Hans Zimmer's company, asking for the opportunity to undertake work experience, and they agreed, so the determined Scot paid his own fare to Los Angeles and the rest, as they say . . .

Lorne is now a Grammy award winner, best known for Dreamworks' animation *Megamind* and Ron Howard film *The Dilemma*, in collaboration with Mr Zimmer. His impressive CV also includes *The Simpsons Movie*, *Angels & Demons*, *Iron Man*, and *Transformers: Revenge of the Fallen*. He also contributed additional music to 2009 Golden Globe-nominated film *Frost/Nixon*, while his role as score producer on 2008's *The Dark Knight* earned him a Grammy for 'Best Score Soundtrack Album for a Motion Picture'.

He wrote the music for top-selling console game *Call of Duty: Modern Warfare 2* and produced the score for Guy Ritchie's *Sherlock Holmes*, which earned a 2010 Oscar nomination. Twelve months later, he worked on Christopher Nolan's *Inception*, which brought another Oscar nomination. The movie starred Leonardo DiCaprio and Michael Caine.

But despite achieving Hollywood success, Lorne insists on working from Scotland at his Highland studio, and while pitching for *River City*, which, he revealed, was influenced by the work of Big Country's Stuart Adamson, he said, 'One of the main reasons I am so keen to win the Scottish soap commission is to highlight the wealth of talent there is in Scotland.

'I think the BBC were surprised that I submitted eighteen pitches instead of just one, but they gave me three weeks so I just kept coming up with new ideas.'

So next time you watch the programme, just remember the Hollywood link!

By this time, we had a catchy theme tune, incredible set and many hours of exciting scripts – all that was now required was a group of between twenty and twenty-five characters to bring the show to life. And there was no shortage of actors willing to throw their hat in the ring for the high-profile gig, yet only a lucky few were successful in landing a role on the Scottish soap.

CHAPTER 2

Meet the Neighbours

They are the people who put the heart and soul into Montego Street. The army of characters who have kept us entertained for the last decade. Here, you can find out exactly what makes them tick. Which one of your favourite characters was a pole dancer in *Emmerdale*, or who sold pies for a living at a Scottish Premier League football stadium. And talking of football, which character who portrayed a top star couldn't even head the ball properly? And discover which character quit his job in a cake factory to become an actor. And did one budding hairdresser really wear a pair of slippers to her audition in Shieldinch?

MEET THE NEIGHBOURS

Many folk have passed through the riverside port of Shieldinch during the last ten years. Some stick around, some move on quickly and others, like Lenny, decide to stay even though they're clearly not welcome. Here we take a look at some of the major characters and the people behind them.

Cormac O'Sullivan (Jason Pitt) 2002–2005

Jason remembers getting the call from his agent, instructing him to be at a Glasgow audition the next day to try out for the part of an angry Irish chef – just out the nick for manslaughter. He wasn't mad keen as he knew those casting the part would have plenty of Irish actors to see, and who were far better at the accent than him. Another call said they'd settle for regional English!

The following day didn't start at all well. When he arrived at Gatwick Airport, his flight ticket was under the name of Mr Jason 'Titt' – but he insisted the audition went well! He said, 'I didn't think I'd get it because all the actors up for the part looked far more like how I imagined Cormac to be. But I went back for a recall a few days later and worked with director Jim Shields, who really put me through the mill. It was a joy to be tested.

Serving up a treat…
Cormac O'Sullivan (Jason Pitt)

'I was told the part was mine and was delighted, but I was living on the south coast of England and knew I would be some distance from my family. But actors have to go where the work is, earn a few quid, and I already knew and loved the city, having previously worked in theatre in Glasgow.'

But Jason reckons he might have felt somewhat different had he known he would be sticking around for three years. 'The good thing about the geography of it all, although everyone I met in Scotland was always pleased to see me, was to be able to step back over the border into England and not be recognised.'

Jason admits he liked Cormac. 'He had many great qualities. He was brave, loyal, tough and trustworthy, and took no nonsense from anyone. He was definitely someone you would have wanted on your side, although he constantly had his finger hovering above the self-destruct button.

'I look back on my time at *River City* with great fondness. I enjoyed the work and all that rare camera time and reckon I'm better at what I do as a result. I met some good friends and loved living in Glasgow and, yes, I miss it a lot.'

But Jason recalled the night he fancied a pizza and jumped on his motorbike to a takeaway in Partick. He said, 'I had only been in the pizza place five minutes when a lady came in saying some neds were wheeling a motorbike up the road.

'I rushed out and saw five or six lads, and my bike, heading towards a Transit van with open rear doors. Even though I knew it could turn nasty, I couldn't just do nothing. I shouted at them and three of them turned, walked back towards me, playing the big men, and asked if I wanted my bike nicked and my head kicked in. I stood my ground.

'Next minute, one of them said, "Ach, no way! You're that big Cormac fella off the telly. How the (bleep) are you, mate?"

'He said, "My mum loves you, big man, so she does. So do I an' all. You need to beat the crap out that Lewis Cope, by the way."

'He went back to the van with a big smile on his face and instructed his mates to "take Cormac's motorbike" out the van. I signed a few autographs and we all wished each other the best and parted company.'

Enjoying her job . . . Hazel Donachie (Annmarie Fulton)

Hazel Donachie (Annmarie Fulton) 2002–2006
Annmarie learned her craft with a local youth theatre group before landing a part in Ken Loach flick *Sweet Sixteen*. The talented starlet attended the

Cannes premiere of the movie then made the seamless switch from single mum Chantelle to Greenpeace-loving Hazel in *River City*, where she had to deal with the brutal murder of her dad (mum died pre-show) and the break-up of her marriage.

It had all started so innocently, with schoolgirl Hazel finding her biggest enemy in step-sister Kirsty. At the time, Annmarie said, 'Kirsty and I were total opposites and didn't ever try to get on.'

After leaving *River City*, she said, 'Since leaving college I've been lucky with my acting career. *River City* provided an incredible grounding and was a tremendous learning process. I'm glad the BBC gave the show time to find its feet as it has gone from strength to strength.'

Roisin McIntyre (Joyce Falconer) 2002–2007

To those running River City in the early days, Joyce Falconer was character twenty-five. To half-a-million viewers, she was Roisin, the lady with the crazy accent who 'bided' somewhere north of Perth. That place was Torry, in the city of Aberdeen, but before making an indelible mark on Shieldinch, Joyce performed mostly in local backcourts.

She explained, 'I was brought up in a housing estate and enjoyed performing fae a young age. My sisters, pals and masel were ay making up oor ain plays, puppet shows and songs. We never had any problems entertainin' oorsels.'

After leaving Torry Academy, Joyce won a place at RSAMD in Glasgow and graduated in 1991. Before 'becoming' Roisin, she had a number of jobs, including papergirl, pie seller at Pittodrie, usherette, singing telegram and balloon seller at the Barras!

After that, she eked out a living as a jobbing actress in plays, panto and role-play for mental health and social work. The life of a budding actor was far from glamorous. Eventually she auditioned for the part of Roisin, who was unrelated to any of the core families, and said, 'I already knew Paul Samson (Raymond Henderson) as a cheeky monkey, so there was natural banter between us. I was ecstatic when I got the job.'

Although Roisin featured in episode one, her first line wasn't delivered until the following show. She recalled, 'Roisin bawls across the street to Raymond from the doorway of Lazy Ray's, "You've a face that would turn milk!" A relationship was born!'

Then came the episode where Roisin accidentally shot former lover J.P. Joyce recalled, 'By this point the public were becoming familiar with me and folk would bawl "RAAAYMOND!" at me in the street. They were fascinated with my accent.

'Roisin's journey was then a rollercoaster. Engaged to Raymond after a slow burn love/hate romance; mine host at The Tall Ship and Deli owner.

'She fell pregnant, had a termination and was reunited with her daughter Alanna, whom she'd had when she was sixteen but had given up for adoption.

'The wedding to Raymond was a grand affair and Roisin used a passage from *Wuthering Heights* for her vows. She'd always been an avid reader of classics, especially behind the counter at Lazy Ray's.'

In the Christmas special, Roisin discovered that Alanna's adoptive father had been abusing her, which culminated in a massive explosion in the caravan. Roisin was injured in the blast, suffered post-traumatic stress disorder and was packed off to a psychiatric institution.

On her return, sisters Shona and Iona had been introduced to help run the Deli. She divorced Raymond and discovered her sister Shona had been sleeping with him. Devastated, she left to go on a cruise.

Joyce sighed. 'That was the end of my full-time contract at *River City*. Since then I've returned with my American sugar daddy, Sonny, as a figment of Raymond's imagination and finally for the funeral of Shona. Who knows if Roisin will ever return to Shieldinch, but according to the public she's nae deid.

'I miss the camaraderie with my colleagues and a laugh with the crew. I think Roisin's impact was mainly due to my use of broad Scots, which folk are unused to hearing on television. She was witty, blunt and tough but had a heart of gold and enjoyed some cracking one-liners.

'I could have never imagined how it would affect my life. I have done a lot of varied work since leaving Shieldinch but have had to accept in some folk's eyes that I will ay be mad Roisin – her wi the voice!"

Alice Henderson (Lorraine McIntosh) 2002–2008

Despite spending many hours with her face stuck in a vodka bottle, Lorraine McIntosh looks back on her five years at Shieldinch fondly. From day one when she returned from a father-imposed exile in London, until she finally left Montego Street humbled and drunk as a skunk, Alice proved one of the show's pivotal characters. Along the way, we were treated to the classic HIV storyline, the night she was so drunk she 'allegedly' slept with Shellsuit Bob, and her jail sentence for downloading child porn. Ms Henderson was rarely idle.

Tortured…Alice Henderson (Lorraine McIntosh)

Despite major parts in *Taggart* and the lead in stage play *Men Should Weep*, Lorraine reckons the part of downtrodden Alice was her biggest acting break.

Best known as part of perennial Scots chart-toppers Deacon Blue, she revealed how she still gets cries of 'Has Alice stopped drinking yet?' during gigs! She said, 'I remember all the talk of a Scottish soap and thinking what a brilliant opportunity it would be for so many actors and crew. My son was two at the time and in terms of home life/ work balance, it was perfect, but I didn't think it would ever happen.'

Lorraine auditioned for the part three times and eventually received a call from her agent saying, 'Congratulations Alice!' But Alice was 'held back' for around eight weeks and introduced as an impact character, although this led to Lorraine getting it in the neck from her 'brother'.

She explained, 'Paul Samson, who played Raymond, had read in the papers that I was being brought in to "save the dying soap". As if! He soon realised that wasn't down to me.

'Alice was an interesting character and great to play, but soap is like no other genre, where you can see the beginning and end of your character's trajectory, which was quite difficult at times. Playing an alcoholic wasn't something I took on lightly. You have a duty to interpret the character as realistically as possible and John Murtagh, who played my dad George, was very helpful. As a former alcoholic he had been through the twelve steps to recovery.'

Once the apple of her father's eye, Alice had gone off the rails and had a child at sixteen before veering towards the dark side of life. If Alice couldn't be George's precious little daughter then she wasn't wanted. 'It was a brilliant back story,' said Lorraine. 'She comes back after all those years and expects everything to be the same, but Derek is sixteen and has a mind of his own.'

Alice soon turned to drink and hit an all-time low when she 'slept' with her son's best pal. 'I still cringe at that storyline,' laughed Lorraine. 'Beforehand, Stephen Purdon, who plays Bob, came up to me and said, "Lorraine, we need to talk about this, we've got a kissing scene coming up."

'I thought, "Oh, no, he's just a kid." Before the scene, he said to me, "Don't worry, I've brushed my teeth." It was a great ice-breaker, and he followed it up by saying, "All my pals think I'm dead lucky getting to kiss that bird out of Deacon Blue!" How can you follow that?'

Lorraine was famed for injecting every ounce of energy into emotionally demanding scenes and admits to more often than not coming off set completely drained. 'The moment I challenged my partner, Mac, over sleeping with young Zoe was just so exhausting. I'm an emotional person at the best of times.

'The death of my on-screen father was also sad, but beautiful. He had his whole family – who had called a truce – around him as he passed away. It was very moving.'

Alice struggled to handle George's death and danced with many demons before finally leaving the show. Her family had simply had enough of her drinking and when she made yet another scene in The Tall Ship, she was cast aside like a leper.

'I loved my time at *River City* and got to work alongside a lot of great people. Alice was an interesting character, to say the least. Even if I hadn't been written out, it was still time to go. We'd covered everything with Alice and it was quite a journey – although it was a sad day when she was eventually killed off.'

'Playing an alcoholic wasn't something I took on lightly. You have a duty to interpret the character as realistically as possible and John Murtagh, who played my dad George, was very helpful. As a former alcoholic he had been through the twelve steps to recovery.'

Celebration: 150th ep. Bob and Scarlett with George Henderson and Jo Rossi

MEET THE ADAMS FAMILY

They're creepy and they're kooky...the Adams Family. Of all the families to inhabit Shieldinch in the last ten years, the Adamses are no doubt the most popular and have provided viewers with hours of entertainment due to their laugh-a-minute antics.

We've looked on as Paddy, Stevie and Madonna have, at various stages, joined Scarlett, Jimmy, Bob and Kelly-Marie for the wackiest journey in soap . . . and it ain't over yet.

Bob Adams (Stephen Purdon) 2002–

Stephen will never forget *that* moment – when he snogged the singer from chart-topping Scots band Deacon Blue, and it wasn't Ricky Ross! Alice Henderson (Lorraine McIntosh) was back on the bevy and Shellsuit Bob popped up with a few cans . . .

Stephen said, 'It was a terrible thing to do to your best mate! But me and his maw had a wee drink, danced to some soppy music and enjoyed a snog on the couch.'

It was definitely a case of 'sofa' so good for Bob, but difficult with dozens of crew looking on. 'I was really nervous the night before and a mate of mine, a massive Deacon Blue fan, was totally jealous. It was my first ever on-screen kiss, and with a real pop star! Lorraine was absolutely brilliant about the whole thing, probably because I'd brushed my teeth EIGHT times.'

But Deek had his revenge. Stephen recalled, 'He caught up with me outside my house. I tried to run but went crashing down the stairs – courtesy of the most amazing stunt "lassie" you've ever seen.

'The camera cut to me lying at the foot of the stairs, blood pouring from a nasty head wound. Cue the heart-tugging "Bob in a coma" storyline! No lines to learn for a couple of months, but the bed sores were murder!'

Back to real life, and Stephen began his journey as a teenage member of the Toon Speak Theatre Group, from Royston in Glasgow. He came across future *River City* casting agent Victoria Beattie and when the part of Shellsuit Bob came up, he got the call.

He said, 'I had just missed out on lead roles in *Sweet Sixteen* and *Ratcatcher* and was at a low ebb, so getting *River City* was great, although it was initially a three-month part.'

The viewing public took to Shellsuit Bob instantly. He soon had a surname, and then a mum, sister and brother. The Adams family was born.

'I fell in love with the character straight away. I knew so many people just like him. He was a loveable rogue. Three months has turned into ten years and it's just the best job in the world.'

Gordon McCorkell, who plays Bob's best friend Deek, has taken that role into real life, just like the rest of the Adams clan. 'We

Domestic bliss . . . Deek and Bob in their caravan

The glamorous Adams family

all get on so well,' he said. 'It's a bonkers family but I wouldn't have it any other way. Directors must dread the Adamses getting together. It's always a bit of a riot!'

But life was rocky for Stephen last year when he was struck down with a mystery brain bug and there were real fears for his health. He said, 'I got the fright of my life. I'm always working and if it's not *River City*, I'm doing panto, and then I like to head off on holiday with my wife, Nicola.'

But after a weekend in Dublin, Stephen collapsed at home and was rushed to the Royal Infirmary. It was the stuff of nightmares. 'Recovery was slow and I wasn't allowed to do anything. No work, football, golf, and no driving. Being inactive isn't me but it was a small price to pay for getting better. Everyone was great and the big boss, Graeme Gordon, visited and assured me that my job was safe.'

Wedding day with Bob, Stella, Deek and Gabriel

But Stephen laughed, 'I got to marry Stella on Valentine's Day, which was probably payback for all the heartache they've put me through. 'Despite being cleaned out by Michelle, dumped by Zara and left at the altar by Charlie, I've had ten fantastic years in Shieldinch, and hopefully the journey isn't finished yet.'

Shellsuit's Top Five Funnies:

1. Bob and Deek stole Ruth's clothes at Lazy Ray's while she was topping up her tan. She had to cover up with a bin bag to protect her modesty.
2. Bob slated Brian for hanging around with Scott. In revenge, Scott pretended to fancy Bob, and the wee man ran a mile.
3. Bob proposed to Michelle with a ring from a Christmas cracker.
4. Deek moved into Bob's messy caravan and established a rota. When Deek went to the pub instead of going straight home from work, Bob served up his dinner – in The Tall Ship.
5. Bob decided to investigate reports that prostitutes had taken over Lazy Ray's. Angela was aware of his intentions, and caught him with his pants down.

Scarlett Mullen (Sally Howitt) 2003–

Sally reckons Jimmy and Scarlett are the Jack and Vera of Shieldinch. The *Coronation Street* duo were the life and soul of Weatherfield for years, and the Montego Street equivalent are something similar.

Scarlett arrived in Shieldinch in her ice cream van in 2003, and the rest of the brood weren't too far behind. She said, 'It has been some journey and I'd like to think there are a few miles left in the "dream team" yet. Jimmy and I really are like Jack and Vera in so many ways. We get on well, fight like cat and dog, but along with the serious stuff we have also enjoyed some great comedy moments.

'And it's all down to Shellsuit Bob being such a great and infectious wee character. If he hadn't been so good there wouldn't have been a call for his family!'

River City was just a few months old when producers started casting for Scarlett, but Sally had been there before. On day one, she auditioned for Eileen and recalled sitting next to the successful Deirdre Davis. Next up it was the part of Heather, and again Sally was sat right next to Jenni Keenan Green. 'It was definitely third time lucky,' laughed Sally. 'I remember Stephen Purdon sitting at the "top table" and we clicked straight away. They must have liked the chemistry.

'At first I thought I'd get a couple of months, maybe six tops, but nine years . . . incredible. It has changed my life. Beforehand it was a couple of days here, a couple there, and a stint at the call centre in between.

Looking good, Scarlett

'Now I'm playing the most amazing, funniest and most fiery character that ever walked the earth. In fact, I think it would kill me to play a calm and relaxed character.'

On the ovarian cancer story, Sally said, 'I knew we had to get it right with both the writing and performance. The writers certainly played their part and I hope I did the same. I was later approached by many people who had been touched by cancer, and they insisted I had done it proud. A doctor whom I met in a supermarket said exactly the same.'

But the gruelling shoot took its toll and Sally revealed how, along with Billy McElhaney, who plays Jimmy, they struggled to complete the scene where Jimmy shaved her hair off. She said, 'That was really tough because it's so symbolic of the disease, but one wee wifey came up to me in the street and said, "Listen hen, you really need to ditch that wig, it does nothin' for ye!" That's the great Glasgow humour for you.

'But Scarlett has also had her share of fun and who wouldn't have enjoyed snogging the gorgeous Billy Davis when we had our little DVD scam going? But one of my favourite storylines was the Shieldinch Stalker stuff because Michael Learmonth, the bad guy, was so amazing.

'So for a wee character that was never out her ice cream van for the first few weeks, to a woman who has been through the mill and some, it has been quite a journey. But it's a great place to come to every day. I had a small part in *EastEnders* a number of years ago and Shieldinch beats Albert Square hands down.'

Kelly-Marie Adams (Carmen Pieraccini) 2003–

In an ideal world, Carmen would be swimming with dolphins and not hanging around Montego Street as feisty Kelly-Marie Adams. Shellsuit Bob's cheeky, gum-chewing sister made an immediate impact in Shieldinch, although when her 'pregnancy' ruse with infertile Billy Davis was rumbled, it brought her down a peg or two.

Carmen said, 'Kelly has left three times, to go to Monaco with footballer Andrew, for pastures new with Father Michael, and swanned off to Peru to "find herself", but the lure of Shieldinch is always too strong to resist.

'When I was younger, I was desperate to be a marine biologist and studied science so hard at school it hurt! But it wasn't my strongest subject and I switched to acting, which I also enjoyed.

'I was born and brought up in Paisley and attended a drama group in Dalry. It was great fun and when the whole idea of being a marine biologist had gone, I took drama at Langside College in Glasgow.

'My dad backed me 100 per cent and encouraged me to do "what would make me happy", which was great.'

Carmen landed her first TV role in the BBC's *G-Force* when she was seventeen. It was filmed at Canniesburn Hospital in Glasgow and ran for three years. She said. 'I then went for the part of Kelly-Marie in 2002 and had three recalls, along with Cas Harkins, who played my brother, Stevie.

'When I was younger, I was desperate to be a marine biologist and studied science so hard at school it hurt! But it wasn't my strongest subject and I switched to acting'

It was weird though, as there were three sets of Kelly-Maries and Stevies!'

Carmen initially signed a two-year contract and said, 'Being an Adams has been brilliant, and I've been really fortunate with my "relations" because we all get on so well.'

When Kelly returned at the tail end of last year, she had company in the shape of little Callum, the result of a fling with Ewan Murdoch. Carmen said, 'I work with kids a lot through the charity Hearts and Minds so being around them is second nature. Robbie, who plays Cal, is lovely and so well behaved. He holds my hand when asked but gets bored quite easy, like us all I suppose.

'It was a stroke of genius bringing the Adamses and Murdochs together through Callum.'

While 'in Peru', Carmen worked on Glasgow comedy *Dear Green Place*, although she is better known for her role as Kelly. Recognition was never part of the master plan though. 'I didn't get into acting for that reason. I love acting – it's the best job in the world – but sometimes the recognition side can be a curse, especially when people have had a wee bit too much to drink!

'But I'm so proud of *River City*. When I'm a wee granny I can look back on it with fond memories, although that won't be for a while yet!'

Going away. Kelly (Carmen Pieraccini) receives flowers from producer Sandra McIver

Stella Adams (Keira Lucchesi) 2009–

Troubled Stella finally got a break from her dismal past when she married Bob in a hush-hush service on Valentine's Day. It was the happy storyline she craved after surviving homelessness and alcoholism and enduring a visit from a mum unlikely to win parent of the year.

But there's more than a touch of irony that she ended up with Bob and not Deek, given both enjoyed an almost identical theatrical upbringing.

Newlyweds Bob and Stella

They started out as members of Paisley theatre group PACE, responsible for spawning talented duo Paolo Nutini and James McAvoy, and were soon appearing in *Chewin' the Fat*. Oh, and both were born and brought up in Barrhead, near Glasgow! 'But I moved to Glasgow when I was five,' laughed Keira.

Keira described herself as 'talkative' and revealed how her mum put her into PACE because she wouldn't shut up. 'I think she just wanted peace and quiet, but I enjoyed it and soon realised I wanted to be an actor.'

She added, 'I was at PACE till I was sixteen, although I got my first acting job when I was nine. It was with the BBC and I played a Jewish evacuee. I also appeared at the Citizens' Theatre and took kids' acting classes. *Chewin' the Fat* was next and I did a bit of presenting for BBC Scotland's *You Cool Live*.'

Keira achieved Higher Drama at school, Lourdes Secondary, but had to move several miles away to try for her Advanced Higher. She said, 'Lourdes didn't offer Advanced Higher Drama so I moved to St Ninian's in Giffnock, but it wasn't for me. I left and tried unsuccessfully for three years to get into drama school.

'In hindsight, drama school probably wasn't for me and it's no great disappointment that I didn't get in.'

Keira was desperate for a role in *River City* and first auditioned for the part of Jennifer Bowie, Charlie's sister. Unsuccessful, she was then put up for the part of Hayley the hairdresser, so it was a case of third time lucky when she got Stella. 'That was a great moment,' she reflected, 'and I've learned so much at *River City*, like the speed you have to work at, which drama school simply couldn't have taught me.

'You need to learn the ropes very quickly, although it's a great comfort having so many talented people, both in front of, and behind, the camera, to help you out.'

Keira insisted that Bob and Scarlett's Valentine's Day marriage was brilliant but didn't give her the urge to run out and tie the knot in real life. 'I'm still young, live at home and in no rush to get hitched for real. One wedding is enough to cope with, although I didn't have a ceremony because we skipped off and got married somewhere secret. So much of a secret, in fact, I still don't know where it was!

Bad boy turned 'good' . . . Vader

'And it was just great to see Bob finally make it through a wedding, especially after the debacle with Charlie when he was jilted at the altar!'

Vader (Ryan Fletcher) 2004–2006

They say you're better being lucky than good. Ryan Fletcher, who played reformed gang member Vader, can genuinely lay claim to being both. Ryan, from Blantyre in Lanarkshire, received the call to join *River City* while he still had a year to go at drama school. He managed to keep tabs on his studies while filming in Dumbarton. It also turned out to be the best career move he's made to date – although that wasn't the way it was meant to be.

Initially, Ryan joined for just four episodes, playing a despised rival of teen troublemakers Deek and Shellsuit Bob. Vader and his crew arrived on set, did their bit and left. No fuss. He said, 'I was attending RSAMD in Glasgow and was asked if I would like to audition for the part of Vader. I didn't need to be asked twice. Shabana (Zara Malik) was in my class at drama school so it was a double success for the RSAMD.

'It was a great experience and while it was just four episodes, it was good to get a foot in the door, because you never know what it can lead to.'

What it led to for Ryan was a fantastic opportunity. Gordon McCorkell (Deek) fell ill and had been scheduled, along with Stephen Purdon (Bob), to take advantage of the Shieldinch Strangler escaping from jail by showing 'tourists' round his old haunts. A decision was taken to re-jig the scenes and find another actor to play alongside Stephen. Ryan was that man. He said, 'Gordon had been bitten by an insect and was really struggling. No one likes to get their break in those circumstances but, equally, you have to grab it when it comes along.

Vader with crew in background

'It all went well and I was in Shieldinch to stay, even though my initial script still had Gordon's name on it!'

Ryan added, 'At first Vader was a bit of a menace, then he became something of a loveable rogue. In fact, it turned out my real name was Courtney Campbell. How bad was that?'

It was one juicy storyline after another for Ryan. The 'homeless' story was massive and then the thrilling love triangle involving Hazel, whom he married, and Alanna, daughter of pub owner Roisin. But it all ended in tears, literally.

Ryan said, 'After a glut of interesting storylines it felt like my final months were spent pulling pints in The Tall Ship.'

The frustrated young actor pleaded for something a bit more challenging than bar work but Vader had pulled his last pint. He recalled, 'I was gutted, but life goes on and I decided to make the most of it. *River City* had given me my big chance and I was determined not to waste it.

'Soap is a fantastic learning curve. Without the experience I would never have gone on to play other more challenging roles. The crew are first class at *River City* and help was always at hand.'

Nicki Cullen (Jayd Johnson) 2004–2010

This girl got off to a bad start in Shieldinch when her 'mum' died on day one, but struck gold when Alice the alcoholic and Mac, a lover of young girls, took her in! Thankfully she had prostitute sister Zoe to turn to. Poor kid!

Jayd was a breath of fresh air and was involved in many gritty storylines, none more so than 'the kidnap'. She said, 'That was my favourite. It was so frightening because Maurice Roeves (Robert) is such a great actor that

I actually thought he was going to hurt us!

'Getting to work with Barbara Rafferty (Shirley) was brilliant, but my favourite character was Lenny Murdoch. He's amazing and another great baddie!'

Jayd left Shieldinch in 2010 to go to New York to study acting at the American Academy of Dramatic Art. She said, 'I always wanted to study in either Glasgow or London, but it was Laura McMonagle, who played my sister Zoe in *River City*, who suggested New York. I thought, "Why not?"'

But at the start of year two Jayd was offered a part in BBC drama *Field of Blood*. She accepted, which was just as well, as she won a coveted BAFTA for her performance.

And Jayd hasn't looked back, although she will always have a special place in her heart for Shieldinch. She said, 'You always remember your first big job, but *River City* was more than that – I loved it to bits!'

Della Davis (Katie McEwan) 2003–2005, 2007

Katie initially trained as a nursery teacher before studying at Manchester Metropolitan University for a BA in acting. Her first TV job was 'Candy', a pole dancer on *Emmerdale*. 'Yes, it was racy,' said Katie, 'but Mum encouraged me to become an actor when I had talked about changing professions.

Nicki (Jayd Johnson), left, with Amber (Lorna Anderson)

Della (Katie McEwan)

'After *Emmerdale* and prior to playing Della, I was a regular on *A&E*, a hospital drama for Granada, and worked alongside Martin Shaw and Niamh Cusack for four years.'

Katie's *River City* audition was a nightmare. 'I was based down south but was asked to Dumbarton for an audition and had to be there early next morning. There were no flights available and the train I was given a ticket for didn't exist. I managed to organise travel, print scripts, pack etc., but the journey was utter madness. I had to change trains twice and was re-routed around every passing tree from London to Glasgow. It was full and noisy, there was no heating or buffet . . . so reading the script was a nightmare. Cold, hungry and everyone screaming in my ears. At my audition I had a rant at the sheer absurdity of my journey, the inefficiency of it all, and if, as actors, we were as competent as British Rail, how we would never work again. I got the job and it was the start of a lovely relationship!'

Billy Davis (Gray O'Brien) 2003–2007

Gray was voted Best Villain at the 2009 British Soap Awards for his portrayal of Tony Gordon in *Coronation Street* – but he was previously

a man behaving badly in Shieldinch. Who could forget *that* game of poker when Billy lost a night of passion with his wife, Della, to the equally nasty Lewis Cope? Or when he tried to keep a baby he found in the portacabin just to get back in Della's good books?

When Gray joined *River City* in 2003, he had just finished a three-year stint on *Peak Practice*, with a spell on *Casualty* already behind him. He was touted as the show's 'marquee signing'.

He enjoyed life in Montego Street and said, 'Billy started off as a bit of a rogue and perhaps lost his way a little. Tony Gordon, on the other hand, took the "bad guy" to a new level. Actors love playing villains and I can completely understand why – it's really good fun.'

During his *River City* tenure, Gray found time to star alongside David Tennant and Kylie Minogue in the 2007 Christmas episode of *Doctor Who*.

But it was as a loveable villain that *River City* fans will remember him. The Flash Harry who seemed to have it all but in reality had nothing at all.

Billy Davis (Gray O'Brien)

Tina Hunter (Jenny Ryan) 2005–2008

Jenny always dreamed of being an actor – quite literally! Long-suffering 'Tina Hunter' started out with the Edinburgh Youth Theatre in her home city, which proved the perfect grounding for a year's foundation course in drama at Telford College. She then attended the Royal Scottish Academy of Music and Drama and said, 'It all came together after RSAMD. It had to, mind, because I had just been

Tina Hunter (Jenny Ryan)

paid off from my job in a Benetton clothes shop – for daydreaming!'

Jenny looked back on her time in Shieldinch with great fondness, and said, '*River City* was great but would've been even better if I could've had more happiness!'

Tina found out her husband was gay and then both her sons went off the rails. 'My favourite story was probably Tina's short-lived romance with Billy Davis. It was the only time she was allowed to be happy, but even that didn't last too long.

'But I'm still incredibly proud to have been a part of a show that so many people enjoy, even if I did end up in Mull!'

Andrew Murray (Sam Heughan) 2005–2006

Theatre-goer Sam moved to Edinburgh from Dumfries when he was just twelve and later enjoyed work experience as a stagehand. He then landed a couple of small parts and was accepted for RSAMD. 'It felt like home,' he laughed.

Sam filmed *Alexander* in Egypt and Greece, and had several adventures stateside before heading back to Blighty to hook up with TAG for the play *Knives and Hens*. 'I got *River City* at the same time,' Sam explained, 'which was difficult because I needed long hair and a beard for the play! I did both and the "Murray Mullet" was born!'

Sam played pro footballer Andrew Murray, Kelly-Marie's squeeze, but insisted, 'Football isn't my strongest skill, but having Andrew play for Livingston at least avoided one difficult conflict of interest.

'While in London, I'd watched *River City* on Sky, and Carmen (Kelly) was amazing. I was warned a few times by Glaswegians, "Look after her or else!"

'I have no idea how Andrew's career is going in Monaco, but I imagine not too well as he loved the high-life. He did love Kelly very much though.'

Andrew Murray (Sam Heughan), with Kelly-Marie

Iona McIntyre

The not-so-new 'new' girl in town,
Jo Rossi (Lisa Gardner)

Iona McIntyre (Claire Knight) 2006–2012

Edinburgh-born Claire was hooked on acting after watching her brother play the Lion in *The Wizard of Oz*. Despite teachers insisting acting wasn't a 'real job,' she stuck at it. 'I had a part in *Hiawatha* when I was fifteen and loved it.' Years later she auditioned for the part of Ruth Rossi in *River City* and, in her mind, she was perfect for the job, having previously played a Gaelic-singing madwoman!

'I left Queen Margaret College in 1998 and played many Edinburgh Festival shows before auditioning for *River City* in 2002. I was recalled along with others (including Morag Calder) for the part of Ruth, but obviously I was unsuccessful!'

A few years later Claire auditioned for the part of Shona alongside Julie Duncanson, and joked with her about being cast as sisters. 'Julie got the part but six weeks later, I was breaking open the champers when I won the role of Iona!'

She added, 'I loved the scenes when the three McIntyre sisters were together. I miss them so much! I'm so proud of *River City*. It's an incredible achievement for a television programme to run every week for ten years and keep its audience entertained.

'I love Iona to bits but the success of the show is down to the loyalty of its viewers and the commitment of everyone directly involved.'

Joanne Rossi #1 (Allison McKenzie) 2002–2007

Allison was the first actress to play the ditzy but manipulative blonde bombshell Jo Rossi and was soon embroiled in some edgy storylines, such as having it off with Nazir under his desk in the computer shop Blinc Inc., having the baby on the landing of her lover's close, being implicated in the murder of Marcus McKenzie, stabbed by his demented daughter, and participating in an affair with her 'brother' – and just about every eligible bachelor in Montego Street. Needless to say, it was a busy time for Allison.

Allison said, 'In the early days of the show, Jo craved fame and fortune, and it didn't really matter whether that was as a singer, actress or model.'

Allison moved to London at twenty-two after landing the part of Sally Bowles in stage smash *Cabaret* at the Royal Court Theatre, and was invited to LA by the agent of *X-Files* star David

Duchovny, but decided to stay put. Movies such as *Club Le Monde* and *Loved Alone* followed, and when *River City* came along she contributed many emotionally-charged performances.

But the very nature of Jo Rossi's loose-cannon character meant a departure at some stage was always likely. And so it came to pass that Jo had what she believed to be her brother, Luca's, baby and the couple were forced to leave town when the whole sordid affair was dragged out into the open. Yet the fiery Jo couldn't stay gone for long . . . And in stepped the second actress to play Joanne Rossi in 2008.

Joanne Rossi #2 (Lisa Gardner) 2008–2011

Lisa Gardner was stepping into a big pair of high heels when she won the right to play Shieldinch superbitch Joanne Rossi. Allison McKenzie had initially made the role her own with a string of stunning performances as 'train wreck' Jo, but a reluctance to return on her part left the door open for a 'second coming'.

Lisa said, 'I was doing theatre at the time and the only television work on my CV was *Sea of Souls*, so I was pretty nervous but excited at the same time. Thankfully I got the job and it was decided I should play Jo my way. It would've been impossible to play the character Allison's way but thankfully producers decided they didn't want a copycat actress.

'I knew a fair bit about the character, but other cast members and crew still knew Jo better than me. She had been through so much but I could only play the storylines I had in front of me.

'Morag Calder (Ruth) was fantastic and a real tower of strength, while the likes of

The original Ms Rossi, Allison McKenzie

Johnny Beattie (my granddad!) and Libby McArthur (Mum, Gina) were also fantastic, especially when it came to the harrowing storylines.'

One such storyline centred on Jo's loss of her son Franco in a car accident that also killed the child's dad, Nazir. Lisa, who hails from the Ayrshire town of Largs, said, 'That was a particularly sensitive storyline and one of the hardest I've ever had to deal with. It's unfathomable how a woman would feel after losing her child. You've nothing to draw on – but something you have to get right.

'We have a real sense of responsibility to the audience. I had people come up to me in the street and say, "I really don't know what to say, it must be awful." That was me acting, so think how difficult it would be if it actually happened to someone you knew.

'The public perception of Jo changed after that storyline. Beforehand, people would tell me how much of a bitch I was, in a jokey way of course, but there was definitely sympathy towards "my" Jo.'

And, of course, desperate Jo then faked pregnancy and miscarriage to keep Ewan. 'That was also really difficult, but I reckon Jo genuinely believed she had lost a baby, because of her emotional state.

'It's with storylines such as these that you draw on the support of your fellow actors, and I definitely did with the car crash and miscarriage plots.'

The last we saw of Jo, she left Shieldinch on the arm of Leo Brodie after a failed romance with his brother Gabriel. Once again, Jo had given her heart far too easily. 'She thought she could mould Gabriel into the person she wanted, but it didn't quite go according to plan, and she paid the price. I believe Jo did love Gabriel and maybe one day she will return to break up Gabriel and whoever he's with!'

Lisa left Shieldinch for a fresh challenge, and said, 'It was my decision. I wanted to do more theatre and moving to London seemed the obvious choice. Hopefully I can return one day and put a few more noses out of joint – Jo definitely has more feathers to ruffle in Shieldinch!'

Liz Hamilton (Eileen McCallum) 2005–

Eileen McCallum will never forget the day she was handed her first *River City* script. It made her laugh so much she just had to move to Shieldinch. Eileen was duly unveiled as Liz Buchanan, upper-crust mum of the evil Archie, and future son killer!

Scotland's First Lady of Soap was now an integral part of her third drama serial, following lengthy stints on Scottish Television soaps *Garnock Way* and *High Road*. She said, 'When *River City* was first being mentioned, I had just left *High Road* and joined the Royal Shakespeare Company, and when I came back to Scotland, the writing was on the wall

for the good folk of Glendarroch. I appeared in shows such as *New Tricks* and *Casualty*, and had started a stint in theatre, but when I was sent the *River City* script – it was wonderful. Liz Buchanan was a fantastic character, a real breath of fresh air. Her son, Archie, turned out to be a real bad egg, but Liz is such a terrible snob and great fun to play.'

After much to-ing and throwing (off cliffs?), Liz settled down as a constant companion, and now wife, for Malcolm, and Eileen admitted that Johnny Beattie is a delight to work with. 'Malcolm and Liz are happy teaching each other new things. They are both such strong characters but Johnny, the man behind Malcolm, is great to work with and is sharp as a tack.'

She laughed. 'He could give me a few years but never forgets his lines and often prompts me. I'd like to think we work very well together.'

Eileen delved into her box of memories to recall the day she landed a part in *Garnock Way*, a 1970s soap based on a small mining community halfway between Glasgow and Edinburgh. She remembered, 'We were toiling as a family and I was working at the Lyceum Theatre with Rikki Fulton. I was called to the stage manager's cubicle where my agent, Freddie Young, said, "Scottish Television want you for their new soap opera."

'I burst into tears. A regular job so close to my Edinburgh home was a dream come true. My family have always been priority so the job security was such a relief. I love the theatre but you can be away from home for such long periods.

'Then it was on to *High Road* and now *River City*. It's great being part of a soap family again and we have such a strong cast. Any one character can be handed major storylines at any given time.'

Eileen revealed that seeing the famous *River City* backlot gave her goosebumps. 'It's so fantastic. I've long been a fan of art departments and what they can achieve. When I first set eyes on the backlot I was stunned.'

And the new Mrs Hamilton insisted she will continue to act as long as she enjoys it and producers want her! 'I am still enjoying myself and it really is a part of my life that I'm loathe to give up. It reminds you that you still have value.'

Niamh Corrigan (Frances Healy) 2006–2007

Born in Limerick, Ireland, Frances had done it all by the time she arrived in Montego Street to plot revenge on nasty Archie for leaving her rotting in jail. She had been a hairdresser, played in a brass band, caught the acting bug and landed her first role as a sixth-century nun!

Niamh Corrigan
(Frances Healy)

Frances said, 'I had a real knack for cutting hair but tried so hard not to ask people if they were going anywhere nice on holiday! But I always wanted to act and got myself into all kinds of variety shows at school. I was in Limerick City Brass Band, where I played drums and euphonium!'

Frances then had a gorgeous daughter, Maria, and slinked into 'mammy mode' for several years. She said, 'Maria grew up fast so I joined a theatre company.'

Frances, an accomplished stand-up, won a place at Trinity College Dublin and was thrilled to get the part in *River City*. She said, 'I loved playing a baddie and working with Eileen McCallum. She is smart and a great laugh.

'I had some great storylines and getting involved with Archie was fantastic. I had waited years to get revenge, but fell head over heels for him – again! I hated lying to Liz but when Niamh decided to help Archie abscond, there was no way back for her.

'It was a wrench to leave but I get bored really easily and am comfortable with change. I love the saying "arrive late and leave early", but I made many friends and left with brilliant memories.'

Sharon McLaren (Sarah McArdie) 2008–2009

Sharon McLaren from Arran waltzed into Shieldinch and stole Raymond's heart – and all his money! It was the first time the Lanark girl had ever played a baddie, and boy did she have fun.

Sarah moved south when she was eight but returned to Scotland for her *River City* role. She said, 'I studied English and Theatre at Warwick University, then had a one-woman cabaret show which toured the UK.' And she played the daughter of Paul Nicholas in hit theatre show *Mixed Feelings*.

Sarah also has many artistic siblings, including brothers, Brian, who played Councillor Alex Judd in *River City*, and Martin, a writer. But regarding her own role in the show, she said, 'I had never played a bitch so I was excited. I was always told I had a baby face and cast as the "nice girl". Sharon certainly wasn't that. I got the job after a third audition and my favourite storyline was stealing Raymond's money and leaving him stranded at the airport, although I felt guilty!

'Working with Deirdre Davis (Eileen) was brilliant and I enjoyed returning a few months later but was frustrated when Raymond pulled the wool over my eyes! Am I still in jail? Will I ever get out?

'It was sad to leave and people still ask if I'm happy with Raymond's money. That's the power of *River City*.'

Sharon McLaren
(Sarah McArdie)

Shirley Henderson (Barbara Rafferty) 2004–2009

Anyone capable of putting up with grumpy George Henderson deserves a medal . . . or a nice life in Spain. Shirley got the latter when she left Shieldinch to live with daughter Della. Initially though, she'd knocked back Malcolm's friendly advances, and plumped for his best mate George.

Before Shieldinch, Barbara was regularly on our screens, but best known for her role in *Rab C. Nesbitt* as long-suffering Ella Cotter. She was brought up in Glasgow and was in the civil service prior to switching careers. 'I had always wanted to be an actress and trained at the Royal Scottish Academy of Music and Drama. My first job was at the BBC in *This Man Craig*.'

Barbara then hung out with Rab C. and Jamesy Cotter for a few years and was delighted when the BBC cast her in the role of Shirley. She said, 'I worked alongside a lot of good people at *River City* and particularly liked the hostage situation with Nicki and Robert. It was intense but enjoyable.

'It was hard to leave but I'm very proud to have been part of it and, who knows, I may even return one day from Spain!'

Shirley Henderson
(Barbara Rafferty)

THE MURDOCH MOLLS

Lydia Murdoch (Jacqueline Leonard) 2007–2011

When you're a Murdoch, you enjoy the lifestyle and don't ask questions. At least that's the way it was for Lydia, until she'd had enough of hubby's shenanigans.

Being born in Blackpool meant Jacqueline Leonard should have been used to rollercoasters, but nothing could've prepared her for life in Shieldinch as the wife of gangster Lenny – not even a two-year stint at *EastEnders*, with part of that spent as Grant Mitchell's other half.

'Being a Murdoch was great though,' insisted Jacqueline. 'We had a great family – all different types but a great mix – and it worked really well. Frank Gallagher (Lenny) is just fantastic to work with and we got on so well.'

Jacqueline fell into acting by default because, after performing well at school in Bonnybridge, near Falkirk, where she was brought up from the age of ten, she headed for art school. But a couple of shows in the West End of London convinced her to pursue acting and she enrolled at the London Academy of Music and Dramatic Arts. At the end of her three-year course, she moved to Colchester in Essex where she appeared on stage in *The Taming of the Shrew*.

She said, 'My first major television work was *Peak Practice*, where I stayed for four series, and I had a stint as David Wicks' first wife in *EastEnders*. I was there two years and loved it, although it was quite hectic at times. I also went out with Grant Mitchell and thought that afterwards I might settle down and take a "gentler" role – then I met and married Lenny!'

Jacqueline laughed. 'Gray O'Brien joined *Peak Practice* just after I'd left and then he was in *River City*. Come to think of it, he's followed me around quite a bit, so I thought I would try and get him back. I was up for the role of Rovers Return landlady Stella in *Coronation Street* but lost out to Michelle Collins.'

But being the wife of such an infamous hood had its baggage, as Jacqueline soon

Empire . . . Lydia at Hola

discovered. 'People would stop me and ask, "Why are you still married to that Lenny Murdoch?" But it was always positive and people were just so good. As for the show, we always got great storylines and there was never a dull moment in the Murdoch household. But I particularly enjoyed my scenes with Scarlett. When I opened Hola we had some real run-ins, particularly when she had Interjumble and Santa's Grotto.

'I'll always remember the grand opening of Hola. We were all inside sipping champagne and nibbling on canapés while Scarlett was outside with her placard staging a one-woman protest against this gangster's moll. It was hilarious and really watchable. The light-hearted element helped take us away from the heavy Murdoch storylines of gangsters and shady business deals.

'But I also loved the whole business with my son Ewan falling off the scaffolding, although that doesn't quite sound right! It was so well done and proved *River City* really could compete with the network soaps.'

Jacqueline is back down south and admitted she only left Montego Street because her daughter was nearing school age and she didn't want to miss out. 'I'm so glad I did it. These moments are precious and don't last long so I had to take advantage of it, but I would never rule out a return to Shieldinch. Lydia definitely has unfinished business!'

Amber Murdoch (Lorna Anderson)

Amber Murdoch (Lorna Anderson) 2007–2011

If ever proof were required that Lenny Murdoch really is a big softie, look no further than his pampered daughter Amber. The baby of the family was at boarding school until the age of sixteen before 'demanding' to live with the family in that 'Shieldinch dump!' Of course, Lenny and Lydia granted her wish and the original and best Montego Street minx was born.

Lorna said, 'It was great playing a little madam, and definitely one that knew how to "work" her dad. I don't think anyone outside of the Murdochs liked Amber but all she wanted was to be part of a family.'

Lorna, who has three brothers, was born in Rutherglen, but the Anderson family moved to Monkton, in Ayrshire, when she was just ten, to escape school bullying.

Her mum was in the Salvation Army and that was where the budding actress first performed in public, in both the choir and drama section.

Family friends marked her down as a little performer from a young age, but the moment she attended her first musical theatre shows, including *Joseph* and *Phantom*, Lorna was hooked. However, her career path was still to be determined. 'I loved musical theatre but was still undecided which career to pursue, even in sixth year at school.'

Lorna enrolled at Langside College on a three-year acting course and was accepted after a three-day audition. 'I knew it was for me,' she said. On leaving college, Lorna picked up an agent, and her first audition was for the part of Amber. 'I was twenty at the time and loved the part so much.'

'I used to go over to my gran's and help with the housework. She was disabled and we would watch *River City*. She would say to me, "One day you will be on that show, Lorna." I hope I made her proud.

'Being a Murdoch was just the best experience. At first I was a bit intimidated by Lenny and his eyes of steel, but he really was a big teddy bear and yes, Amber could wrap him round her little finger!

'At *River City* I grew not only as an actor but also as a person. Working alongside my "mum and dad", Jacqui Leonard and Frank Gallagher, was amazing. If you can't learn from these guys you never will.

'We had some great storylines, but my on-screen brother Ewan's death, and the aftermath, was the most dramatic of all. When I got the scripts I just thought, "Wow", it was so powerful. It was the same with

Nicole Brodie (Holly Jack)

the McCabe shooting, which ultimately led to my exit. These were draining scenes to film, but also fulfilling.

'My entire *River City* experience was the best. It was a definite learning curve because I had only ever worked in theatre beforehand. You become so disciplined and discover so much about acting because it's such a well-oiled machine. And who knows? Amber didn't die so there is always the chance she could come back one day. Whatever happens, my experience in Shieldinch was all positive.'

Nicole Brodie (Holly Jack) 2010–

Holly, who plays minxy Nicole Brodie, went straight from school in her hometown of Airdrie to study musical theatre at the age of sixteen. Her first paid acting job was a reconstruction for *Crimewatch*, then a few months later she endured

an unsuccessful audition for *River City*.

She said, 'When I heard I hadn't got the part I was gutted. Now I'm glad I didn't because my next *River City* audition was for Nicole. As soon as I read for Nicole I loved it – she's such a great character to play.'

Holly insists she wasn't anything like Nicole, who loves indulging in verbal catfights with her step-mum's niece, Zinnie.

'I was a relatively well-behaved teenager but now I get to play out all Nicole's mischief. It's good fun. I've had great storylines – in fact, too many good ones to choose from!'

Like trying to seduce Charlie, Nick Morrison and finally Stuart, which made sense of the old adage, 'If at first you don't succeed . . .' because she soon got her claws into Stevie – before being kidnapped and subjected to a terrifying ordeal.

But despite still being at school, fiery Nicole has certainly marked herself down as a future matriarch – putting her step-mum, Leyla, through the emotional wringer when she discovered her cheating on Michael.

Gabriel Brodie (Garry Sweeney) 2010–

Nicole's uncle and man-about-town, Gabriel, showed his wicked side by 'copping off' with his sister-in-law Leyla.

Actor Garry Sweeney was born and brought up on the south side of Glasgow and lived a stone's throw from former *Taggart* star Mark McManus. Before becoming an actor, he worked in a bakery in Torquay, but his interest in the arts began at Holyrood Secondary School and was sparked by drama teacher Allan Black, who saved him from a 'life on the darker side'!

Gabriel Brodie (Garry Sweeney)

He said, 'My first acting job was in David Hayman film *The Near Room*, where I played a younger version of the main character.

'I got the break on *River City* because I'd known Graeme Gordon (series producer) and he felt I'd be perfect for Gabriel – although I still had to go through a screen test!'

Garry rates the murder of McCabe and the 'whodunnit' aftermath as his favourite storyline. He added, 'I love working with Frank Gallagher (Lenny) and Andy Clark (Michael), but there isn't an actor on the show that I don't enjoy working with.

'*River City* is a Scottish institution and one of the only home-based dramas filmed north of the border. It really is fantastic.'

Bob O'Hara (Tom Urie) 2009–

Tom was brought up in Paisley with best pal Gerard Butler, but when he was just five the family moved to another part of town, and Tom found new friends! He studied rock music and earned cash as a nightclub DJ while penning jingles for radio. Musically, he has been playing Scott Joplin's 'The Entertainer' on the piano from the age of three.

Tom fell into acting by mistake. He was playing piano for the *Chewin' the Fat* guys at their live King's Theatre show and was invited to join the cast for two series of the popular sketch show. He added the *Karen Dunbar Show*, *Only an Excuse* and *Still Game* to his CV.

He joined *River City* in September of 2009 as Big Bob, uncle of Shellsuit Bob, and when thinking back to being offered this role he said, 'It was a dream come true because I'd watched the show since day one.

'I'm also the show's resident musician, so I get to act and perform at the same time.'

Bob O'Hara (Tom Urie)

Tom co-wrote a song for Susan Boyle called 'Never Been Kissed'. 'I tried so hard to get it to her,' he said, 'but didn't manage. Though I've since performed it on *River City* for Iona, so it wasn't wasted. I also released my debut album earlier this year, which was another fantastic milestone. I really do have the best of both worlds.'

Hayley McCrone (Pamela Byrne) 2009–2012

Pamela auditioned for the part of hairdresser Hayley on Tuesday – and started shooting the following Monday. Now that's what I call a whirlwind introduction to your first television job!

'I agree,' said Pamela. 'I trained in musical theatre but thought it would be good experience to go for an audition for television – and I got the part, although I still can't believe how quickly it all happened.'

And Pamela revealed how she wore a pair of 'slippers' to her audition. 'I thought they were Ugg boots,' she laughed, 'it was only when I got home and my mum asked why I had slippers on that I realised what I'd done!'

Pamela learned hairdressing etiquette from fellow cast member John Comerford (Jack Paterson), a real-life hairdresser, and some of her best memories stemmed from that experience. 'I enjoyed it when Jack and Hayley had a fling and also when my character got a severe beating from

Hayley McCrone (Pamela Byrne)

nasty Theresa. I remember going home with all these bruises and Mum thinking I'd been in a nasty accident!'

Pamela has a university degree in philosophy but insisted that appearing in *River City* fulfilled all her dreams. 'Since I was little I enjoyed singing and dancing and musical theatre was my passion, but being involved in a highly-successful television show was so amazing.'

Sadly, Pamela filmed her final scenes in April of this year, and we saw the last of Hayley in July. She said, 'It wasn't my decision to go and I was really sad to leave, but these things happen in television.'

Stevie Burns (Paul James Corrigan) 2011–

Paul found it anything but a piece of cake getting a job on *River City*, but the moment ex-addict Stevie Burns showed up in town, he vowed to stay as long as possible. And he has since had more than his fair share of juicy storylines.

'Initially I was in for three episodes, caused a bit of havoc with Raymond, and left, quick as a flash.' But producers liked what they saw and Paul was asked back, although at the time he was rehearsing for a pantomime in Stirling. 'That wasn't going to stop me taking the gig and we worked round it.'

So far, we've witnessed Stevie make several valiant attempts to stay off heroin despite being placed in an impossible but priceless situation. His girlfriend Nicole Brodie was head over heels for Stevie, but her dad Michael, the local GP, had a 'not on my beat' attitude to his work. Paul said, 'In a way, Stevie was Michael's success story. The doc was running an anti-drugs programme and Stevie managed to beat the habit and stay clean – until he relapsed! On the other hand, Stevie was going out with Michael's daughter, and that's an absolute no-no.'

The moment Paul arrived at *River City*, he knew he had made the right decision some years previously when he quit his nine-to-five to pursue a dream. The Bellshill boy worked in a nearby cake factory and was used to permanently smelling of chocolate and jam! However, he had always harboured an interest in acting but was unaware of how to take the next step until a work colleague told him about an acting course at Coatbridge College.

'I filled in the form but received a call while I was on the conveyor belt filling cakes with jam. "We have an audition for you today at 1.30pm." I told them I was working and couldn't make it and that was that. But when I really thought about it, I knew I had to be there, so I walked straight out of the factory and headed for the college.

'They asked me to perform a monologue, but I didn't know what that was. I was way out my depth and decided to head back to the cake factory, but the course leader stopped me. He explained everything and gave me thirty minutes to prepare. I read a sequence from the Bruce Willis film *Twelve Monkeys* and was eventually offered a place on the three-year acting course.

'What it has led to has been phenomenal and I wouldn't be on *River City* had I not had the courage to walk straight off the production line.'

He added, 'Stevie's a loveable rogue, but when I was told I would be playing a reformed addict, I did a lot of research because I wanted to get it spot on. There are a lot of parents out there who can identify with what he's going through.

'I was delighted to get such a big storyline. Producers obviously thought I could pull it off, which was a massive vote of confidence.

'There was also the issue of Nicole being underage and them sleeping together, but I like to think we portrayed that in a responsible manner because Nicole was on the pill and Stevie got a health check at the surgery. The last thing we wanted to do was send out irresponsible messages.

'But filming the scenes where Nicole went missing was really hard. I was walking round the backlot, looking at all these "missing" posters. It was really sad.

'I've been in loads of scenes with Holly Jack, who plays Nicole, and she's brilliant to work with. We were brought up not far from one another but had never met, although we soon hit it off.'

Stevie has tried many things to 'fit in', such as doing DIY for Malcolm, but has a battle on his hands to be accepted by some of the more staid members of the community. I have a feeling, though, that he's not a quitter.

These are just some of the past and present custodians of Shieldinch but, like any other continuing drama, new faces will appear at regular intervals and, sadly, many stalwarts will leave town – never to return!

Stevie Burns (Paul James Corrigan) with Holly jack

CHAPTER 3

Shieldinch

Most of the action in Montego Street happens in the pub or café. Here, we take a stroll round the local area and call in on those who make their living out of providing a service to residents.

Bird's eye view of Shieldinch

SHIELDINCH

Most soaps are constructed around the staple public meeting place, such as a pub, café or salon. Shieldinch has all three – and many more. Here we show some of the key sets and information about the individuals who run them.

Raymond lost in thought

The Tall Ship Proprietor: Raymond Henderson (Paul Samson)

Paul has spent a chunk of his life behind bars, so from the moment in episode one when his alter-ego Raymond was kicked out of The Tall Ship, you just knew the Shieldinch boozer would at some stage become the centre of his universe.

Following the murder of Tommy Donachie, Raymond was soon lording it over drinkers when his wife Roisin bought the pub from her lottery winnings – all a far cry from the low-level crook that owned Lazy Ray's in the early days. Paul said, 'Raymond was initially turned on by the shady side of life, but he was soon behind the bar at the Ship, which was perfect from my point of view. I'm a pub man and spent half my life serving behind the bar. I took it as a compliment and a measure of the trust the production team had in me. Some of soap's biggest mainstays are behind bars, if you know what I mean!'

But Paul was ready to quit acting just before *River City* started and had promised that if he didn't get the gig, he would walk away. He said, 'I was approaching forty and acting can be a tough game when you start hitting the likes of thirty-five. I was making reasonable money but stability was zero and *River City* was the last chance saloon.'

He remembered, 'They were looking for four lead parts – Tommy, Eileen, Gina and Raymond – and the fingers were crossed. When the call came through to say I had the job, I was delighted and booked a holiday. For once in my life that stability was there.'

But Paul remembers the dark days when there were calls for the BBC to cut their losses and pull the show. 'From the word "go" the broadsheets didn't give us a chance, but we had the support of the BBC and that was the main thing. We knew it would take time to consolidate and didn't feel we were given that chance by some people. Now we're ten years old and it feels wonderful, but it's not about saying "I told you so". That was forgotten a long time ago.

'I like to think I've played a small part in the show's success, although my weddings – all four of them – have taken up quite a bit of air time. Okay, so I was already married – and divorced – to Eileen when the show started, but it still counts!

'Raymond's a real optimist, and a true romantic at heart. He always tries to do the right thing, although whether or not he succeeds is open for debate. He split up with Roisin because he promised to keep quiet about her daughter Alanna's lap-dancing.

'My two weddings to Shona were a little misguided, and then there are the relationships with Heather and Sharon, but it always seems to come back to me and Eileen – she's like my bossy big sister!

'The show has been a great success and I think that's partly down to real-life characters that speak native tongues. People in Scotland used to cringe when they heard the Scots accent on TV, but I think that's changed now.

'It has been a fantastic ten years and I'm so proud of what really is a wonderful show.'

Proprietor of The Grill (part of The Tall Ship): Eileen Hamilton (Deirdre Davis)

Whisper it, but Deirdre Davis is happy that in ten years of *River City*, Eileen has never once had a birthday to celebrate so, technically, she is still thirty-seven! Of course, the downside is a lack of tasty cake to munch, but she'll live with that.

Eileen Hamilton

Best known for her flings and relationships with younger men, as well as keeping big sister Gina in check, Eileen has been at the heart of many a meaty Montego Street storyline, and she's not finished yet. But rewind ten years and like the majority of the Scottish acting frat, Deirdre was quick off the mark when word filtered through that a Scottish soap was in the offing. It was the big break many craved but few achieved – Deirdre was one of the lucky ones.

She said, 'It turned out to be a life-changing job for me. For an actor to be in steady work for a decade is unheard of – and I'm still the same age ten years on!'

Oh, and don't forget the conquests, which we've lost count of. We've had Tommy Donachie; Lewis Cope; Dr Vinnie Shah; Callum Stuart; Liam the chef; Archie Buchanan; Councillor Alex Judd; Murray Crozier; Annie's ex-man, Sandy; a brief flirtation with Father Dominic and a series of moonlit trysts with Raymond, the last of which produced baby Stuart. Not great for a woman's reputation. Deirdre agreed, and said, 'It was sheer hell having to get up early in the morning knowing that I had to snog hot young guys like Donald Pirie (Callum) and Patrick Mulvey (Liam) at work! Seriously though, it makes it so much easier if you're working with people you like, and both guys were fantastic.

'But I'll never forget the relationship with Lewis Cope. The affair was at its height when we stopped filming for the year. After the winter break, we picked up the story at exactly the same point but in real time it was a couple of months later – and I was eleven weeks pregnant. It was meant to be just a couple of hours later but I had changed beyond recognition. I couldn't get near my continuity dressing gown, and it looked as though someone had inflated my face with a bicycle pump!'

But Eileen always seemed to head

Fed up . . . Eileen and Murray Crozier (Brian Cowan) 'enjoy' the great outdoors

back to good old Raymondo, one-time love of her life and father of her three children, one of whom, Kirsty, is dead, while Brian is currently in a mental institution. Let's hope for better things for young Stuart, then!

Deirdre loved the botched Gina/Archie/Liz murder attempt, in which she became a major player. 'At that time, Eileen was probably at her meanest. She would walk all over Gina and just sleep with her men. She was horrible.

'I also enjoyed filming the camping storyline with Gina and Murray. We were in this field, up to our knees in mud, but it was great fun.

'And I will never forget the introduction of the Adams family. Scarlett turned up in her ice cream van and within minutes was out shouting at Gina. That was hilarious.'

Deirdre added, 'We seem to have a winning combination at *River City* and the show is loved by everyone from the young to the elderly. And I'm blessed to have Johnny Beattie for a dad. He may be the elder statesman but he has more stamina than the rest of us put together!'

Proprietor of The Oyster Café: Gina Hamilton (Libby McArthur)

The year 2012 was the year Gina finally emerged from the shadows of her bossy wee sister Eileen, and boy how we loved it. For years, the eldest Hamilton sibling had looked on with a large dollop of resignation as Eileen ruled the roost. Man-eating Eileen scoffed at the very thought of Archie fancying Gina, so she had her wicked way with him, then coerced Gina into making a romantic meal for her and new flame Murray, and ended up chasing the community centre worker straight into big sis's arms.

Gina Hamilton

But times have changed and Libby admitted that despite having justifiable reservations about Gina's second coming, she has enjoyed the renaissance of a character once regarded as the Shieldinch doormat. She said, 'I adore Gina. In fact, everyone loves humble Gina because she is so trusting. Ask her to steal a purse and she would tell you to get lost, so if she is going to change, become tougher and stick up for herself then great, but it has to be all or nothing.

'People have expectations of her and she was moulded into a pillar of the community over nine years. It's a long time but that's who she became, although I now like to call her "leaner, meaner Gina!"'

The very thought of Gina standing up to Lenny Murdoch a few years ago would have been laughable, unless, of course, he had hurt her family. By doing so, she earned the respect of many. And then there was the time she threw horrible hubby Archie over a cliff! Libby recalled the moment she was told of the controversial storyline, along with cohorts Eileen and

From left: Lenny Murdoch, Gabriel Brodie, Molly O'Hara, and director Jim Shields

Poster advertising Carly's Café

Liz. 'I sat there agog, thinking, "How are we gonna pull this off?" But, you know what, we did, and I think it worked well. And, of course, it was a lot of fun heading down the coast to dispose of Archie's body!

'But any time I'm given the heads-up on a new storyline involving Gina and core cast members such as Malcolm, Eileen, Raymond or Liz, I get excited because we all work well together and as warring siblings, Gina and Eileen have few equals.'

Libby added, 'I'm so grateful to be a part of *River City* because it's brilliant. It has been consistently better than anything else Scottish on our screens for ages and I'm not alone in thinking that.

'It had a tough beginning, but that was down to the Scottish psyche more than anything else. We always slag things off up here, and when it becomes a success we jump on the bandwagon and attach ourselves to it, and that's what I believe happened with *River City*.

'We have enjoyed higher ratings in Scotland than established soaps such as *EastEnders*, and that tells its own story.

'The cast represent the show twenty-four/seven because you are constantly stopped in the street by people wanting to tell you they either love or hate you. People normally want to tell me how much they like Gina, although that's changed a little recently and has been replaced by, "You tell them, love!"

Libby was the only actor to make the initial switch from STV soap *High Road* where she played Senga, the wife of Chic Cherry (Andy Cameron), and insisted the programmes are chalk and cheese. 'I learned so much about television on *High Road*, because a lot of it was shot in the studio with three pedestal cameras, which is completely different from *River City*. That said, the production values on *River City* are far greater and I reckon it represents Glasgow life more, whereas *High Road* was rural.

'Part of the reason for *River City*'s success is the genuine warmth and hospitality of Glaswegians and Glasgow. The time was right for a soap set in Glasgow, and I think we have it spot on. Here's to the next ten years!'

Others with Big Business Interests

Since the opening episode of *River City*, making money has been at the forefront of many a storyline: from Lewis Cope Construction to Tommy's ailing boatyard. Business and its countless opportunities have evolved in tandem with the show's many great characters.

Moda Vida, the first salon in Shieldinch, was opened by Billy Davis, who was later joined in the business by his wife Della. During tough times, Della's mum Shirley bought a stake in the business and later sold the salon rights to Gordon Swan. Gordon opened Just Gordon on the site of Lazy Ray's tanning salon and McGrade & Kydd Solicitors, knocking both premises into one. His daughter Hayley took over the running of the business when he left town.

The Mini Market

Enterprising Derek Henderson saw potential in the old Conway Spices warehouse and gained planning permission to open Deekafe, which was later sold to Carly Fraser, who re-branded it Carly's Café. When Carly left Shieldinch, Lenny Murdoch's daughter Amber opened her own cab business in the premises, which Lenny runs while Ms Murdoch is a guest of Her Majesty.

The corner shop was initially run by the Maliks but was later bought by Roisin when she won the lottery and turned it into a deli. When Roisin left to go on an indefinite world cruise, Raymond kept it going with Iona in charge, but later sold it to a chain who re-opened it as a mini market.

Blinc Inc. was the brainchild of Scott Wallace and Nazir Malik (right), but nasty Heather conned Scott out of the graphic design business and turned it into Versus wine bar. It was later a second-hand shop, which then closed.

Travelling Shieldinch

Shoppers visiting Shieldinch from out of town would use the subway or regular bus service to get to Montego Street or, if they've had a wee win at the bingo the night before, maybe one of Amber's Cabs!

Nazir's Blinc Inc.

New addition . . .
the snowbound subway
station

The fantastic underground station was put to good use when daytime TV host Lorraine Kelly turned up unexpectedly for Gina and Archie's wedding. And while few trains may stop at Shieldinch on their way to Partick and Cowcaddens, it's still a wonderful addition to the set and yet another outlet for directors and writers. On a busy day outside, you can pick up a bunch of flowers, a *Big Issue* or pop your loose change into one of the many charity collection cans.

Adjacent to the station is the taxi rank, for Hackneys only, and once a regular haunt of George Henderson. The rank has witnessed its fair share of tragedy, most notably Fi Kydd's fatal crash, when she was driven, quite literally, to her death by the evil Archie – or was it Douglas?

The wee red bus also took centre stage when the Shieldinch Strangler made an Orson Welles-type entrance before going on to murder big Tommy in the boatshed.

The bus has been stopping across from the Oyster Café since wee Bob was still in a Shellsuit, although the original site for the shelter was directly opposite the Maliks' corner shop. Producers thought it was too near The Tall Ship though. On one occasion, after frighteningly high winds, the crew arrived early in the morning to find the bus shelter halfway down Montego Street!

So the next time you're on public transport, it may be best to make sure the terminus isn't Shieldinch!

Location is Key

Most drama productions rely on exterior scenes to complement studio filming. It breaks up the monotony and claustrophobic feeling of constantly being confined within four walls. In the late 1960s, Scottish Television's first attempt at soap, *High Living*, set within a high-rise block of flats, failed to go the distance for this very reason, while its predecessor, *Garnock Way*, travelled the same, sorry route. *High Road* stood the test of time though, which was in no small way attributed to the spectacular scenery of Loch Lomond, and producers exploited its natural beauty to the full. *River City* has the best of both worlds, with around a dozen or so spacious, practical studio sets being complemented perfectly by a purpose-built backlot. Even then, locations outwith the lot at Dumbarton must be used to add freshness and authenticity to individual storylines. Here, we take a look at a selection of location storylines and how life panned out on the road for the cast and crew of *River City*.

It all started at Greenock Prison as Lewis Cope waited patiently to pick up Cormac O'Sullivan, who was preparing to leave the nick following an eight-year stretch for manslaughter. Filming took place outside the prison gates before the crew packed up and headed for the west end of Glasgow to shoot a sequence of interior shots as the one-time friends talked about the bad old days.

It was then over to the Bellahouston House Hotel, on the south side of Glasgow, for the wedding of Tommy Donachie and Eileen Hamilton. It was an exciting time, and there was much more to come . . .

2003 – SECC & River Clyde, Glasgow: Another dramatic storyline that demanded a change of scenery was the kidnap of Jo's baby Franco. Ewan was in town to help niece Hazel after she was orphaned. Unfortunately he was followed down the A9 by barmy girlfriend, Helen. He snogged Jo at a party, which left Helen fuming.

Days later, Scott was out with Franco when they bumped into Helen, who insisted it was far too cold for the wee one to be out without a hat. Scott foolishly went back to fetch one and Helen swiped the baby. Jo and Cormac tracked her down to the SECC in Glasgow and found the baby

Cheers: Tommy (Eric Barlow) and Eileen, original Tall Ship publicans

in her car. Still convinced Ewan was in fact seeing Jo, the silly mare made quite a splash by jumping into the Clyde.

2003 – Greenock Sheriff Court: Later that year, the crew once again headed off in the direction of Greenock to film Heather's trial for the murder of Marcus McKenzie while the court was closed for the weekend. There was a lot to pack in. The trial itself and the aftermath in which Marcus's equally deranged daughter Steph stabbed Jo in the court foyer. But it all worked out in the end . . . although maybe not for Heather.

2005 – Glasgow city centre & Govan: Hazel kicked Vader out after catching him with Alanna. He was sleeping rough on the mean streets of Glasgow and Hazel, feeling guilty, talked Bob into helping her find him. They handed out flyers and eventually spotted him in a tricky situation with a Glasgow gang. Thug, Mez, lashed out with a knife but caught Hazel, and she was taken to hospital. After her release, things still weren't working out and he left again, but this time Hazel wisely stayed at home!

2005 – Paisley Sheriff Court: Caught downloading child porn onto Mac's computer, Alice was sent for trial! Remorseful Alice spoke up and admitted she had done a terrible thing. A woman scorned, etc. She had craved revenge but while she was full of apologies, it wasn't enough. She was given six months and the family broke down as she was handcuffed and taken down . . . but the crew would soon be back in Paisley to film Archie's embezzlement trial.

2006 – Clydeside: One of the most dramatic outside jobs centred on the kidnap of Shellsuit Bob's girlfriend, Charlie, who was snatched by Lenny after she witnessed him kill Sammy the Snitch in the Shieldinch boatyard.

Lenny threw the hapless cleaner into the back of his van, which was driven to the Clydeside, with gangster McCabe also a prisoner. Once there, the gang awaited the arrival of a consignment of drugs, while Bob and Jimmy hid behind pallets of cargo to await the police.

Lenny exchanged his fake money for drugs and set about killing McCabe but the cops swooped and rounded up his gang. Lenny took Charlie hostage and gallant Bob grabbed the gangster, which allowed Charlie to escape. A furious fight ensued, and Bob and Lenny ended up swimming with fishes in the River Clyde. Harry dived in to save them and Bob was eventually dragged to the surface but there was no sign of life. When he came to, he didn't regret a thing and Charlie told Bob she loved him . . . but was Lenny dead?

Spot of bother . . . Charlie (June Brogan) at the Clydeside

2007 – Eyemouth: The crew made for the south-east of Scotland to film the demise of evil Archie. The episode marked the fifth birthday of the show and saw the three ladies head for the fishing town of Eyemouth to film the dramatic scenes, although they didn't make a very good job of finishing off Mr Buchanan!

2008 – Dumbarton: A housing estate in Dumbarton was the scene for the thrilling storyline which brought rogue cop DCI Whiteside to book. The crew spent an evening filming the exterior shots in which armed cops rushed from waiting vans into the close of undercover cop Jodie Banks as the honeytrap storyline threatened to go wrong.

DCI Eddie Hunter and Harry Black were outside in an unmarked van, staking out the premises and conducting the delicate operation, with Harry eventually donning his SWAT-team gear to lead the assault. No doubt some strange looks from locals when they decided to peek out from behind the curtains to see what all the commotion was about!

Cliff-hanger . . . Eileen and Gina 'unload' Archie!

2008 – Buchlyvie, Stirlingshire: The return of Fi from Millport triggered Douglas/Archie's memory. She had to go. He plied her with vodka at

Solemn . . . Viv (Louise Jameson) and Shirley

McGrade & Kydd, and when he told her he was Archie, she panicked, ran out of the office and into her car. Drunk as a skunk, she crashed straight into a taxi. As they awaited an ambulance, Archie taunted the dying Fi. That was the cue for the cast and crew to head out to a quaint wee church near the village of Buchlyvie, around twenty miles from Dumbarton, to film the funeral.

2008 – Paisley Sheriff Court: Prior to Archie's embezzlement trial, he tricked Gina into renewing their wedding vows on the advice of his solicitor. Eileen refused them the use of the Ship and far-off Ruth was the only guest at the ceremony in her flat.

Jo banned Gina and Archie from Franco's birthday party, but the alienated café owner became suspicious when she saw Archie acting aggressively towards his mum on Scarlett's wedding video.

At the trial, lawyer Charlie Houston put forward a convincing case, especially with neither Gerry nor Fi able to testify, but Gina finally came to her senses, screamed that Archie was a conman and a liar and was dragged out by security. The judge allowed Archie to walk free.

2010 – Balloch: Murray booked a hillwalking 'treat' for Eileen but Gina ended up going in her place. It went well and Murray booked a similar Valentine's treat – for the trio! This time, Gina made her excuses but agreed to drive them to the campsite and had a good laugh at Eileen's inappropriate hiking gear . . . and torn face.

Eileen realised it wasn't for her and phoned Gina to pick them up, but Gina's car broke down and they were forced to camp out for the night – in one tent. In the morning, Eileen was jealous to see Gina and Murray at one with nature and enjoying the great outdoors.

2011 – Central Station, Glasgow: Ruth arrived home from her latest stint in hospital to discover Scott was moving to the Lake District with Victor. A social worker told sad Ruth that Gina had been asking about custody of Eilidh, and Ruth then lost her job at the health centre. She shared a glass of wine with Scott on his last night in Shieldinch and, next morning, Scott said his goodbyes and the tears flowed. Ruth was watching Eilidh sleep when Scott returned. He asked her to go to Cumbria with him and Victor – and she said yes.

Gina refused to give the move her blessing and at the train station, Ruth was visibly upset until Jo turned up to say goodbye. Just as the train was about to leave, Gina arrived and shared a tearful goodbye with Ruth.

2011 – Helensburgh: Big Bob left home after the death of Tatiana's baby but Christina was upset and wanted him back. Nicole, Stevie and Christina found him busking in a Helensburgh street but he insisted he was finished with her and her mum.

Nicole and Stevie used the time away from Shieldinch to get to know each other a wee bit better in the back of Stevie's van, while a sad Christina sat alone with a bottle of cider.

Christina showed Bob the handprint of the stillborn child, but he said it changed nothing. A drunken Christina headed home and had a go at her mum.

It was Hogmanay and everyone gathered outside the Ship for the bells, but as 'Auld Lang Syne' played in the background, Christina heard a familiar voice, and there was Big Bob to give her a bear hug.

So, while Shieldinch may not be everyone's cup of tea, it certainly has its good points and, if you keep your eyes peeled on a Tuesday night between 8pm and 9pm, you might just see a property for sale! House next to the noisy Brodies, anyone?

Ruth and Eilidh in ambulance

Rescued: Christina and Big Bob

CHAPTER 4

Losing the Plot: 10 Years in Shieldinch

It started with a kiss as Tommy and Eileen tied the knot in a private ceremony, but amidst a backdrop of warring siblings and old flames, the marriage had little chance of surviving. Still, the wedding of the year set the scene for a decade of stunning storylines and riveting plots. And it has continued in a similar vein ever since, thanks to the likes of Alice Henderson, Deek's alcoholic mother, who ruffled her fair share of feathers, and handsome Billy Davis, who put his wife through an emotional wringer. Characters young and old have cemented their place in living rooms the length and breadth of the country as we welcome them into our homes each Tuesday night.

The original cast

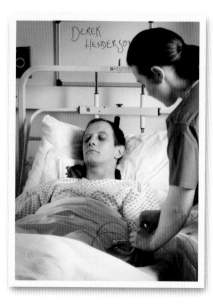

Almost over. Deek in hospital after the crash

Ah, the age-old argument: Is soap driven by character or plot? There's no doubt that strong, believable and interesting characters are a given, but to make the formula succeed, we need stimulating and sustainable storylines that will keep half-a-million viewers hooked and booked for the next episode. To do that, writers and producers must continually come up with fresh plots and seamless transitions, not just 'where were you' moments but storylines that will have viewers discussing the latest scandals and cackling at moments of comedy genius. To 'celebrate' the tenth anniversary of *River City*, viewers will see original character Deek perish in a car crash and The Tall Ship torched by gangsters attempting to cover up the 'murder' of slimy Sean Kennedy.

But the opening night drama began with the wedding of Tommy Donachie and Eileen Hamilton, a match made in hell but a storyline that guaranteed viewers many emotions rolled into one. For starters, there was love but unfortunately for Tommy, Eileen still had a hankering for old flame Lewis Cope. The wedding was chaos and the 'joining' of siblings from the couples' previous marriages was like meteors colliding in the night. Eileen's daughter Kirsty washed step-sister Hazel's favourite white top in with her pinks, while Brian developed an unhealthy obsession for Hazel.

Eileen's ex-hubby Raymond left a nasty message on the happy wedding video and was then unceremoniously booted out of the evening reception. Kirsty fell and banged her head and blamed her step-dad. Happy daze!

But as year one drew to a close and viewing figures tumbled dramatically, producers had an ace up their sleeve – Deacon Blue songbird Lorraine McIntosh, who was introduced as Deek Henderson's long-lost mum. Apparently, George Henderson had paid his daughter to leave sixteen years previously after her life had spiralled out of control due to drink and drugs – and an unplanned pregnancy.

So, Alice was back, drink and drug free and desperate to catch up with her son, although Deek's problems were just beginning. He would also discover the demon drink with best buddy Shellsuit Bob and it wouldn't be long before he was spending more time with his beloved mum – at Alcoholics Anonymous meetings!

There were a couple of bad eggs hanging around Shieldinch but doting grandmother Moira Henderson wasn't one of them. However, George's long-suffering missus was indulging in a little shoplifting – and had a dozen tins of Pledge stashed away in a living room unit. Obviously the not-for-profit strain of kleptomania. Thankfully our streets became so much safer when police arrested this heinous criminal. When Moira was being led into the armoured cop car, though, she spotted grandson Deek and made a run for him. Police assault was added to the growing charge sheet and nasty Moira was given community service, to be served in the heart of Shieldinch. The shame of it all.

'Impact signing' Alice Henderson

New year, new gal in town – and this one was taking lip from no one. The year 2003 saw Scarlett Adams pitch up her ice cream van in Montego Street and daughter Kelly-Marie and son Stevie weren't far behind. Bob and Scarlett were sleeping in the van after being evicted from their council house so they broke into old Lily's house while she was in Canada visiting her son and claimed squatters' rights. It's soapland, and it worked. No one batted an eyelid apart from old

The Adams Family arrive in Shieldinch in style

Malcolm, and no one listened to him. The housewarming spiralled out of control and Bob admitted to girlfriend Zara that his family embarrassed him. Gina complained to Scarlett about the noise. Cue catfight!

Arguably soap's greatest moment arrived when Bob proposed to Zara from a cherry picker with a ring he'd nicked from Lily's. Just a few weeks beforehand, Zara had decided to wear the hijab to school and Bob had insensitively called her a raghead. She was then racially abused by a gang of thugs who had come into the shop to buy drink, and when she tried to chuck them out, they ripped off her hijab – but reformed Bob rode to her rescue.

Dr Marcus McKenzie

Also that year, there was a harrowing storyline in store for faithful viewers, and it centred on mild-mannered Gina. Since the pre-programme death of her husband Franco, she was more interested in serving up cappuccino at the Oyster than men, then along came handsome medic Marcus McKenzie with the perfect chat-up line, 'Your grandson is going to be just fine.' He swept Gina off her feet with a string of romantic dinner dates before deciding it was time for 'dessert'. Gina, though, was content with a kiss and a cuddle.

He wanted to take her for a birthday meal; Gina wanted to spend it with her girls. Ruth unwittingly set the lovebirds up at Gina's cosy little flat and after dinner they enjoyed a slow dance. Marcus handed over an expensive necklace in return for a little lovin'. Gina resisted his charm but the pushy Aussie accused her of leading him on, shoved her onto the bed and had his wicked way.

Marcus (Stefan Dennis) and Heather (Jenni Keenan Green) celebrate the award

Brazen Marcus turned up next day with flowers and was flabbergasted when Gina had the audacity to shun him. Isn't that what she wanted? They met up at baby Franco's party, where Scott noticed Gina acting ultra-nervous around Marcus, and she told him everything.

The following day, though, Gina looked on in horror as Marcus was presented with a Heart of Glasgow award – after being nominated by a completely in-the-dark Jo.

The year 2004 started with a bang – literally. Brian was holding Hazel hostage in the kiltmaker's basement and told her they would be together forever – in death! He locked her in the cellar and chucked her house keys and mobile down a drain, which was spotted by Vader.

Brian nipped over to his gran's to take an overdose but Moira

It's over. Moira's final journey

caught him. He ran out the house and into Della's car, which conveniently had the keys in the ignition. Lightning-quick Moira jumped in beside him but the car smashed into the builder's yard and went up in a ball of flames. Brian emerged relatively unscathed but Moira formed an integral part of the fireball.

Vader turned detective and found Hazel. He proposed, she accepted and George handed over Moira's eternity ring. Vader doesn't mess around – well, that comes later!

Derek had grown up knowing only his gran and granddad – poor kid. But with his mum back in town in 2003, there was just a single piece of the jigsaw missing, but not only was Graeme 'Mac' MacDonald Deek's dad, he also had a few skeletons in a rather packed closet.

Now, let's see. He was Alice's former teacher and lover . . . and her mum Moira's ex-bed partner. Wow! George blew a fuse – as if he needed a reason – and craved revenge. He tracked Mac down to a school

Happy families. Alice (Lorraine McIntosh), Deek, and dad, Mac (Gordon Kennedy)

canteen. When George mentioned baby Deek, the penny dropped – he's the daddy. Graeme soon came looking for his newly discovered offspring – and George tried to run him over. Welcome to Shieldinch!

Deek met his dad and was understandably angry with Alice for keeping him a secret. He then looked on as his dysfunctional parents battled for his affections. Alice bought him a laptop, but Mac had beaten her to the punch, etc.

Gina and Scarlett chatted with Mac and were shocked to discover his wife and son had died in a house fire. Meanwhile, Deek didn't like sharing a flat with Billy and moved in with daddy-kins. Alice invited Mac over for dinner and they ended up snogging, and then George forced Mac to own up to Deek that he'd had an affair with the lad's granny. Deek told Mac, 'You're no father of mine.' Ouch! Deek then dumped Alice. Alice dumped Deek, then got back with Mac. In fact, it was tough trying to remember who was still talking to who at one stage.

Understanding Dr Vinnie Shah was a tad easier, until Alice walked in on him as he was about to inject himself and threatened to report him to the GMC. Vinnie had recently been blackmailed by Zoe, and he returned to the surgery late on, left a message apologising to his parents for being a failure as a doctor, and sobbed before hanging up. He injected himself with a fatal dose of drugs.

Happier times. Vinnie Shah (Archie Lal)

News of Vinnie's death spread through Shieldinch and while Alice felt guilty about the suicide, Mac tried to convince her she did the right thing in reporting him. Vinnie's family arrived looking for answers, and Alice pointed to Zoe's blackmail of Vinnie as a major factor in his suicide. The pair rowed and when Zoe suggested Deek left as a result of Alice's behaviour, she received a slap for her troubles, which was witnessed by a shocked Mac.

The year 2005 brought the most bizarre relationship in Shieldinch, although Harry's first date with Ruth was a disaster. He complimented Jo, and Ruth went nuts. She then spotted him with a glamorous new partner and went nuts again. A pattern? She organised his life and forced him to 'move in', and when he refused to play along, she whacked him. She invented a stalker, called the cops and asked for Harry, because he 'understood' her! It worked, and they kissed.

Ruth bitched to Harry about DCI Hunter and he told her to stop acting like a brat. She thumped him and split his lip, and when he called round to dump her, Ruth said she would decide when it was over. Try a little *Sleeping with the Enemy* and *Single White Female*, add a little *Fatal Attraction* and bingo, you've got yourself a delicious Harry-meets-Ruthie cocktail!

Christmas couldn't be Christmas without a little controversy, but *River City* took it to a new level when Alanna's pervy dad arrived for the festive season and moved into the caravan. Alanna rejected his twisted

All smiles . . . Donna McCabe (Paula Sage) in the Oyster Café

advances and ran to the Ship. Alex tried to light his cigarette using the gas hob but was too drunk to switch it off.

Raymond, Roisin and Alanna stormed across the boatyard to the caravan. Inside, Alex fumbled with his lighter and . . . BOOM. The blast lifted the trio off their feet, and while Raymond and Alanna were conscious, Roisin was taken to hospital in a critical condition. Alex was dead.

Fireball . . . up goes the caravan

Just as controversial a storyline that year was the discovery by Scarlett and Ruth of a young girl with Down's syndrome lying in the middle of Montego Street. Harry found out that Donna's dad was McCabe, although she didn't want anything to do with him. Donna got a job at the Oyster and McCabe spotted what he thought were guys laughing at her, but they were laughing with her. McCabe broke down in front of Scarlett when Donna told him he had never been a father to her. Scarlett helped patch up the relationship and Donna moved in with her dad. Bless.

With Tommy Donachie the show's first major casualty in 2003, it was a further three years before another mainstay was killed off. This time it was grumpy George Henderson, who discovered he had an incurable brain tumour. His 'gal', Shirley, had no idea and when she saw him with his nurse, Jessica, she was convinced he was having an affair. He gathered the family round and was about to tell all when Shirley accused him of the affair. He took a turn.

Raymond called Jessica and Shirley went mad. Jessica revealed her identity and George told everyone he had cancer. He was dying, and as the clan gathered in the Ship at Hogmanay, George proposed. No, not to Jessica!

The year 2006 also revealed

Stolen moment . . . Jo and Luca

that even though Jo was in love with Italian stallion Luca, her 'brother', she agreed to get engaged to her boyfriend, Billy. Naturally, it was a tricky one, but it was all sorted when Luca told Jo he loved her – as a sister. Billy bought Jo a £6,000 diamond engagement ring. Luca who? Luca then confessed to Jo that he loved her . . . but NOT as a sibling, and while dim Billy pressed ahead with his wedding plans Luca and Jo cuddled up in bed.

Evil Archie discovered Luca wasn't actually Jo's brother. Jo was fuming and binned Luca – what, because he wasn't her brother? Archie ordered Luca to leave and made Jo tell her mum that Luca had gone back to his wife and kids in Italy.

When Jo announced she was pregnant, infertile Billy was delighted. Jo confided in Ruth that Billy wasn't the dad. No kidding? It'll all end in tears . . .

Now, why would you call a baby that's born on Christmas Day after a pop star? Beats me, but that's exactly what Jimmy and Scarlett did. Scarlett had kept the happy news from daddy Jimmy till after the scan, but he found out and Scarlett put his gas at a peep by telling him they would never be a couple.

Up in the air...Jimmy hit by joyriders

Ex-criminal Jimmy decided to go straight and bought George's taxi. Scarlett was impressed when he had the names of her children 'tattooed' on the side of his gleaming Hackney.

Scarlett went into labour during the Christmas rush and by the time Jimmy got home, the baby was coming. They rushed to hospital but little Madonna popped out in the back of the cab.

But the sound of baby crying turned into wailing sirens when Jimmy and Scarlett rowed over their future a few months later. Jimmy stormed out and jumped in his cab. Scarlett went after him but he roared off and when his brakes failed, almost hit a woman with a pram. He checked up on the woman but a car full of joyriders came hurtling round the corner and tossed him up in the air like a rag doll. He was taken to hospital where he lay unconscious while Scarlett and prospective new love Terri fretted over him.

Once fit enough to go home, disabled and confined to a wheelchair, Terri was nowhere to be seen, but Scarlett took him back to the Adamses, where he accused

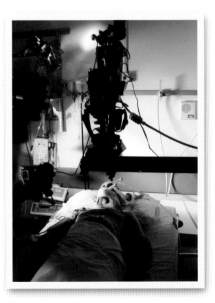

Touch and go...Jimmy in intensive care

Scarlett of pitying him. Raymond built him a gym in a lock-up and Jimmy vowed to walk again. That's the spirit, James.

At George's funeral in 2007, Raymond spoke of how honest his dad had been and Alice butted in by telling all and sundry that George wasn't her dad. She then drunkenly suggested Shirley had poisoned George to get at his brother Robert, and Shirley slapped her. It was the end of the road for the tortured alcoholic. Deek was fed up with her drunken behaviour and threw her out into the street. Shirley stood side-by-side with Deek as Alice staggered out of Shieldinch for good.

Nasty piece of work…
Robert Henderson
(Maurice Roeves)

And then the fun began. Robert turned nasty and wiped George's wedding video, ruined the inauguration of his memorial bench then, to cap it all, took Shirley and Nicki hostage before Billy and Malcolm broke down the door and rescued them – although Nicki copped a sore one when she hit her head against the hall unit. What a send-off.

But there was more drama in store for armchair viewers when nasty, bullying Archie finally got his comeuppance. The shamed lawyer had pushed his mum and Gina to the edge – and they helped him over! The storyline gripped a nation and 'fall-guy' Archie reaped what he had sown.

He was charged with embezzlement, Gina raised bail and he repaid her by sleeping with his nemesis, Niamh. The duo planned to abscond to Acapulco, but Liz and Gina uncovered his plans. He attacked Gina and Liz hit him over the head with an urn – containing his father's ashes! His motionless body lay on the hallway.

Liz, Gina and Eileen drove to a cliff top, pushed the body over the edge and left a suicide note in Archie's car. Racked with guilt, Liz confessed all – but thankfully the cops thought she was nuts!

Escort…Zoe (Laura McMonagle) with pile of cash

Zoe was also heading for a fall, metaphorically speaking. Lenny made a family toast to Rory and Zoe while plotting the shamed hooker's downfall. He offered her £10,000 to leave Shieldinch but when Zoe told

Nicki she was off, little sis decided to tag along. Rory pleaded with her not to go but she chucked him out and when he returned, he found her in bed with Ewan, and a pile of money beside them.

Nicki also saw them and ran off in tears, even though it was a set-up to ease Rory's pain. Zoe left cash for Nicki but she gave it away to strangers in the street, and Rory attacked Ewan. Lydia kicked Ewan out of the family home but a smiling Lenny handed him a set of keys to a posh new flat. Result!

A little light relief arrived in 2008 in the shape of Sonny Munro – Roisin's new squeeze. But when he unveiled plans to open a burger joint in Shieldinch, fuming Shona organised a protest. Sonny's heavies pushed folk around and knocked Scott over. In retaliation, Shona and Carly chained themselves to the railings.

Brothers in arms. Ewan (Chris Brazier) and Rory Murdoch (David Paisley)

Roisin offered her sympathy but Shona blanked her and Scott also snubbed Roisin because his injury was down to Sonny's bully-boys. Iona signed up when Sonny told her no woman could ever beat him.

Contractors tore down the fence, and that was it for Roisin, who joined the protest and brought Sonny's burger empire crashing down. To get back in her good books, Sonny bought her a Highland castle, as you do!

Premature . . . An advert for the ill-fated Sonny Burgers

And scriptwriters also came up with a cracking plot for Ruth – that she had lost it! Shirley, Scott and his boyfriend Manu found her on the floor with a newborn at her side, but Ruth soon slumped into depression. Scott stepped up to the plate, called the baby Eilidh, and was named on the birth certificate as the father.

Gina wanted Eilidh christened but Scott said no – look what religion did to him. Sneaky Gina and Scarlett stole holy water from a church and performed

Rooftop protest, Marty with baby Eilidh

All action, the community centre boxing club

the ceremony as Ruth stared into space. Manu sent Marty a snap of his daughter but when he turned up both Scott and Ruth pretended the baby didn't exist.

He burst in, swiped the baby and ran off, with Ruth in hot pursuit. Marty climbed onto a rooftop and Ruth followed. She told him they could be a family again, took the baby back and ran off. Lenny ran Marty out of Shieldinch.

The year 2009 began with several women being sexually assaulted on the underground, and the hunt was on to find the predator. Hairdresser Jack had scratches. He was in the frame, but was soon freed.

A rather drunk university lecturer, Michael Learmonth, offered to teach Scarlett how to read and she was soon under his spell. Jimmy was suspicious and demanded Scarlett stop seeing him. Naturally, she refused. At a tutorial in Michael's flat, Scarlett realised Michael was the stalker. We already knew, stupid! Michael ushered Scarlett down to the basement (to strangle her) but Jimmy, Bob and Deek arrived in the nick of time and rescued the distressed damsel.

Daniel McKee was back in town and fancied running a boxing club in the community centre, but wife, Marianne was against it – isn't she always? Father Mulvaney backed his plans though and agreed it would teach local kids discipline. Residents soon united against the club so twisted Marianne decided to back Daniel – doesn't she always?

When Daniel headed to London for a youth charity meeting, he left ex-pro Joe in charge. Marianne had her suspicions that Joe was drinking, but matters came to a head when he allowed two boys, Kevin and Rib, to settle their differences in the ring despite the latter having never fought before. Both boys were injured in the dust-up and Joe's 'milk carton' contained whisky. When Daniel returned he was astonished to find Marianne in the ring sparring with Joe. So were we!

The community centre was the new hub of Shieldinch and Councillor Eileen gave her victory speech there. After her election victory, almost-skint Lenny realised ex-councillor Judd was no longer useful but the gangster desperately needed a planning application pushed through. Eileen refused to cooperate so he used money Lydia had saved for Amber's eighteenth to grease Eileen's palms, and it seemed to work.

Impatient to find out how the planning meeting had gone, he followed Eileen into the community centre, where she was making a speech at the launch of Daniel's boxing club. He couldn't believe it when she said, 'And thank you to Lenny for a fantastic donation of £10,000!'

The application had been rejected as the land was worthless, so he threatened Eileen and tried to get his cash back from Daniel, but it was already spent.

And there was more sorrow round the corner for Lenny, who had created a monster by introducing Lydia's long-lost son, Lee, to the family just to get back in his wife's good books. Lee was an imposter and had started to become a nuisance.

In 2010, Lenny told Ewan to dispose of his 'brother' and warned a shocked Lydia that Lee had developed an unhealthy obsession with his 'sister' Amber. She agreed he had to go, although not to meet his maker, and was relieved when she received a text from him, but Ewan had sent it. Lee was still alive – but only just!

Father Mulvaney advised Ewan to tell the police about Lenny's orders but Lenny warned the priest to keep his nose out of his affairs.

It turned out that Ewan had come to Shieldinch to help his real mum, Mary, gain revenge on Lenny for earlier misdemeanours. Lenny soon made Mary, and Archie, disappear. Lenny was onto Ewan and lured him to a flat, where he beat him up. Lydia, Amber and Lee turned up at the door and Lydia tricked Lenny into opening up. A scuffle ensued and Lydia called the police. Ewan scrambled out of the window and onto a scaffolding rig.

Menacing Lenny (Frank Gallagher) in confession

Lenny pleaded with Ewan to get back inside but he slipped and fell to his death. Malcolm saw the entire event, but kept schtum, and Lenny was charged with murder.

When police uncovered two bodies from the boatyard, Mary and Archie, and Lydia told Liz that Lenny had killed Archie, Malcolm told the police he saw Lenny throw Ewan off the scaffolding.

Body count: Archie and Mary's bodies exhumed

Malcolm attended Ewan's funeral with Amber but couldn't meet Lenny's eye. He was a broken man and Liz urged him to tell the truth. Malcolm told the police everything and Lenny was released from jail. He confronted Lydia, who had planned to run away, and held a gun to her head but couldn't pull the trigger.

Lydia left Hola to her daughter, who had hooked up with nasty boy Lee. He was keen to get his claws into both her and the business. He sacked Scarlett, because she wasn't classy enough, and lied to Gordon that Amber wanted to leave the salon to concentrate on the family business.

Lee's controlling behaviour increased, but when he bagged up Lydia's things for chucking out, Amber exploded. She tried to grab one of the bags but Lee turned violent and punched her. He apologised immediately, talked her round and she asked him to stay.

When Jo confronted Amber about Lee's controlling ways, she didn't appreciate the meddling and agreed to go to France with him. On the day of their departure, Jo finally convinced Amber to see sense and she sent him packing and moved in with Malcolm and Liz.

Christmas in The Tall Ship was its usual hoot, although everyone was relieved when moany Eileen sallied off to the toilet. She went into labour though and a drunken Raymond kicked down the door. Jimmy took them to hospital and later on, Raymond and Eileen brought baby Stuart home to a warm welcome in the pub.

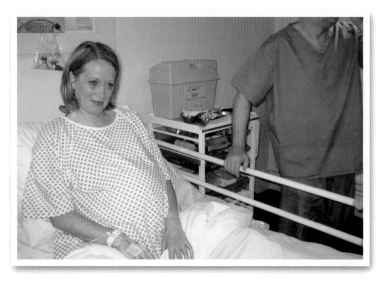

Christmas present: Eileen in maternity

Scarlett's brother, Big Bob, was living next door to her, but his love life was a shambles. Iona laughed when Bob mentioned he was a virgin. He went looking for a prostitute, but the hooker was an undercover cop and he was arrested for soliciting.

When Bob told his brother-in-law, Jimmy, he was horrified, but at least he was the only person that knew. Wrong. The local newspaper carried the story on the front page and nasty Nicole broadcast the news to the whole of Shieldinch (population 28). He then received a dressing down from Molly.

Bad guy McCabe finally met his maker in 2011. He was released from jail and wanted Lenny's head on a plate. His lackeys trashed Hola so Lenny plotted to kill McCabe and turned his daughter against him so she would leave Shieldinch.

McCabe stabbed Jimmy for his part in putting him behind bars and made for the arcade – venue for the rumble. The time for talking was over and Lenny was ready to pull the trigger when his MS kicked in and he dropped the gun. Amber and Fraser rushed in and a shot rang out. McCabe was dead and Amber was holding the gun.

She confessed to the killing, although DI Donald was convinced she was covering for her dad. Off she went to the pokey for a very long time.

Lonely Lenny made the mistake of buying a pretty lady a drink. It was Frances, McCabe's sister, although she 'forgot' to tell that little detail to Mr Murdoch. She was acting on the orders of her evil mum, Agnes, and was to do whatever it took to avenge the death of her brother – and that included sleeping with the enemy.

Collared: Big Bob is arrested for soliciting

Agnes wasn't the only one who wanted Lenny's head on a plate, though. DI Donald was another and he paid Frances a visit, but she had fallen for Lenny and refused to daub him in. A rather frustrated DI Donald tried to force himself upon her. Turned out there was a bit of history there.

DI Donald didn't give up and a few weeks later Frances recorded their tryst and mailed the evidence to her bank – and warned the duped cop to leave Lenny alone.

But when Frances was out with Lenny's grandson, Cal, they met Agnes, who feigned injury. She asked them to escort her back to her care home with her driver, Gus, but she kidnaped the kid and enticed Lenny to McCabe's old home.

Agnes demanded a ransom payment and Gus went with Lenny to collect the cash. Lenny overpowered Gus but Frances told Lenny that Cal was being held in a room that was rigged with explosives, and in turn she had to reveal her true identity. She told him of a way to get Cal out, and he did, successfully.

Agnes took a real turn and Frances left her to die. She begged Lenny for forgiveness but he gave her ten seconds to walk out her life – because he loved her. Her final act was to give DI Donald the info that brought the McCabe empire crashing down – but nothing on Lenny.

'Fire,' screamed the natives of Shieldinch, and while we never actually saw any flames, we knew that trouble lay ahead. The raging inferno took place in the nether regions of the Shieldinch halt and Dr Brodie's crash team awaited the first wave of casualties.

Annie staggered out, but Stella was nowhere to be seen. Cue hulking Gabriel, and he pushed past the emergency services in a bid to get the girl.

Leyla worried for her lover but big Gabe returned moments later holding unconscious Stella and handed her over to waiting paramedics – her wedding dress the only high-profile casualty!

After the last of the casualties had been dealt with, Dr Brodie proposed a drink in the Ship and when Leyla dramatically refused, his response was, 'Well, no one died!' Brilliant.

Dr Dan's gambling was to eventually give grumpy Michael a good reason to scowl – especially as he'd used the practice credit card to play roulette online.

The good doctor was struggling to pay back the £5,000 loan from Lenny Murdoch, as it had quickly morphed into ten grand, and the gangster was putting the squeeze on for his cash. Dr Dan pulled in every penny from every available source but still it wasn't enough to quench Lenny's insatiable thirst.

Meanwhile, Tattie noticed irregular payments had been made to the surgery account and asked Dan if he knew anything about it. Course he did, and he finally fessed up to 'borrowing' the money to feed his gambling habit. Problem was, the accounts were about to be audited and Tattie knew Michael would demand answers.

Dan insisted he was beating his habit and Tattie promised to keep it a secret from Michael – for now. But Lenny was hovering in the background and when the remainder of cash wasn't forthcoming, he demanded Dan get patient records to recompense him. That night, Doc stayed late and got what Lenny wanted, but just as he was about to hand them over, guilt pangs saw him hand them to a baffled Kelly-Marie. He stood up to big bad Lenny and received a tanking for his cheek, but at least his problems were over. Yeah, right.

River City truly became must-see television when Nicole became involved with bad guy/good guy Stevie. They indulged in drinking and under-age sex but the final straw for Nicole – apart from being totally fed up with moody dad Michael – came when she caught step-mum Leyla kissing Uncle Gabriel.

Nicole took off and moved in with Stevie's drug dealer mate Cammy, while Stevie 'tried to get them somewhere to live'. But Stevie was in prison and knew nothing of Nicole's whereabouts.

At a police press conference Michael and Leyla appealed for Nicole to come home, while her best friend Christina was torn between helping Nicole or 'doing the right thing'.

Sadly, Cammy was grooming Nicole for 'sale', although his tortured girlfriend Angie eventually let Nicole go. But the Brodies' troubles were merely beginning, with the good doctor beating Cammy to a pulp. And the price for walking around with a length of lead piping? A murder rap and regular helpings of porridge!

But, thankfully, the fantastic storylines don't end there. Scriptwriters have an endless supply of great plots in the bank, and we can look forward to many more in the coming years.

Please help us find Nicole!

Nicole Brodie was last seen on Montego St, Shieldinch at around 6.30pm on Tuesday 14th February

Aged 16
Slim Build
Shoulder Length
Brown Hair
Brown Eyes

Missing! Family appeal for return of Nicole

CHAPTER 5

Wedding Bells

'I'm getting married in the morning', and plenty of Shieldinch residents have walked down the aisle with the very best of intentions – only for the whole occasion to end in turmoil. Tommy and Eileen started the trend and the latest newlyweds, Malcolm and Liz, will be hoping to avoid a similar fate. In between we have looked on as Raymond, wed to Eileen pre-show, has tried his luck with Roisin and her sister, Shona (twice), and has gone back to the original and best partner. How we enjoyed watching Hazel snatch her twenty minutes of happiness by marrying Vader in Vegas, but we looked on in horror as Jo Rossi was knocked down after Archie and Gina's reception.

WEDDING BELLS

We all love a good wedding and, boy, have the residents of Shieldinch had a few crackers to sink their teeth into over the years. In fact, the nuptials have been flowing freely with no fewer than thirteen weddings taking place since the show started in 2002 – from the opening episode Donachie alliance to Malcolm and Liz's romantic Loch Lomond ceremony. Read on to see which characters got hitched, which weddings went without a glitch – and those who ended up marrying twice, or who just got ditched!

Tommy and Eileen (2002)

Tommy and Eileen's wedding introduced both clans to the show, but the writing was on the wall from the word 'go', and perhaps the Donachies and Hendersons were destined to have an unhappy future. Should Tommy and Eileen have said 'I DON'T'?

Happy couple, Raymond and Roisin

Wedding gamble. Hazel and Vader got married in Vegas

Roisin and Raymond (2004)

Roisin and Raymond set the date for the wedding of the year and

Raymondo headed off in search of the kid that Roisin had given up for adoption in Aberdeen.

Mum and daughter were soon reminiscing over old photos, although, unsurprisingly, the teenager didn't remember too much from those days.

Come the wedding, Roisin was stunning in her dress and Bob stepped in at the last moment to ensure the glamorous bride didn't walk down the aisle alone. The happy couple danced to Proclaimers classic 'Sunshine on Leith' before heading off on honeymoon to Dubai. Just perfect.

Vader and Hazel (2004)

The loved-up couple plumped for a Vegas-style wedding – in Las Vegas – but Vader didn't have a passport. Eileen sorted it, and the couple returned as Mr & Mrs Campbell. Bob gave them a present (a washing-up set) – but only because he wanted to turn Tommy's boatshed into a garage. Hazel agreed.

Ruth and Marty (2005)

Tortured Ruth returned from a soul-searching trip to Italy a married woman. She had met Marty Green in Rome, but Malcolm reckoned Marty was a figment of Ruth's troubled imagination and when Luca phoned the Santa Celeste church in Italy, he was told there hadn't been a wedding there for years.

Ruth, Malcolm and Gina waited in the Ship for Marty but had all but given up when he walked in, straight off the set of *Footballers' Wives* – tanned and dressed to the nines. Malcolm told him of Ruth's 'issues' but he insisted the past didn't matter.

Father Michael led their wedding blessing in The Tall Ship and Ruth was diagnosed with a personality disorder. Really?

Happy couple. Marty and Ruth

Archie and Gina (2006)

On the morning of the wedding, Bob and Charlie bumped into celebrity Lorraine Kelly as she made her way from the subway to meet up with old friend Billy Davis, who had persuaded her to attend the reception. Bob pocketed Lorraine's used champagne glass to sell on eBay while the TV star crammed as many sausage rolls as she could into her handbag.

Grumpy George almost knocked little Franco down in his taxi. Billy saved him but Jo was hit by the vehicle and lay unconscious on the street. At the hospital, medics confirmed that Jo was stable and the baby was fine. Baby, what baby? Billy was delighted and Jo apologised for not telling him sooner. Just another Montego Street marriage!

George and Shirley (2007)

Dying George hastily made his wedding plans. Raymond contacted George's long-lost brother Robert, who was shocked but agreed to visit. The brothers had an emotional reunion but after a heart-to-heart, Robert admitted to having an affair with Moira, although caring George forgave him.

George told a devastated Malcolm of his terminal illness and asked him to be his best man. The wedding was a happy affair until George, spotting Robert and Alice together, stormed over and revealed that Robert was indeed Alice's father. Gasp! And after telling Raymond and Alice they were the two best kids he could've hoped for, he died peacefully in his living room with his family around him.

Raymond and Shona (2007)

Shona ran off with Raymond to get married in secret but her ex-man Tony turned up. The happy couple celebrated tying the knot but Tony told

Raymond that he was still married to Shona. Raymond chased her and it transpired there was also a third husband.

Raymond reported the bigamist to the cops and Harry arrested her. She struggled with life in the nick. Roisin persuaded Raymond to skip court, as the judge needed all THREE of Shona's husbands there. He agreed, until Tony warned him that he could lose his pub licence if he failed to show.

Raymond testified but Gerry noticed that Tony's Bahamas wedding to Shona was illegal! Roisin was raging with Raymond, and Shona tried to talk to him but he was down on himself so Shona went on a cruise with Roisin!

All ended in tears. Raymond and Shona (Julie Duncanson)

Jimmy and Scarlett (2008)

It may have been Jimmy and Scarlett's big day, but crazy Charlie stole the show. Even Charlie's mum advised Bob to ditch plans for a double wedding. Bob dumped her but she pleaded with him and he relented. Tough love, huh Bob!

The big day arrived and an excited Jimmy managed to get up on crutches and tears flowed as he said his vows – the happy couple were married.

Bob stumbled through his vows, but when it was Charlie's turn, she ran off. He chased after her and asked her to go to the reception with him and she agreed, but as Bob read out his speech, Charlie left Shieldinch in a taxi. Once again, Bob was left broken-hearted.

Kiss the bride. Jimmy (Billy McElhaney) and Scarlett

Raymond and Shona (2009)

Shona spotted Sharon and Raymond on CCTV and thought they were an item again, but wily Raymond was setting his ex up for a fall. Raymond and Shona left for a new life but returned and told Iona they were getting married – again. Shona took a dizzy turn and Iona thought she was pregnant.

Shona collapsed on her wedding day and the doctor confirmed a second aneurysm. Raymond was told to prepare for the worst. The couple were

determined to marry and Father Mulvaney performed the ceremony at the hospital. Moments after they were pronounced man and wife, Shona died. She was laid to rest in the family lair on the Isle of Barra.

Never last. Ruth and Andy
Carroll (James Michie)

Ruth and Andy (2010)

Ruth was unhappy so Iona got in touch with Andy – Ruth's ex – but Andy's mum was furious and warned off Ruth. Andy was right behind her – with fiancée Gabriella – and told Ruth he was getting married.

On the morning of the wedding, Andy had second thoughts and Gabriella spotted him share a peck with Ruth outside No. 5. Panicking, she told Andy she was pregnant and he vowed to stand by her.

Ruth burst into the wedding, *Graduate* style, and told Andy she loved him. Gabriella confessed to the phantom pregnancy.

Andy proposed to Ruth, and Jo hired Morna, the 'wedding planner', but she did a runner with the cash. The family procured dresses, a venue and catering but couldn't fix the marriage licence. Ruth was devastated but Jo arranged an unofficial ceremony at the Ship, with Malcolm as registrar.

Big Bob and Tatiana (2011)

Big Bob was a worried man. His suit was too small, then he clocked Iona spill out of a handsome man's car and thought of their kiss the night previous. Iona and Bob met secretly in the beer garden and she insisted they should be together. They shared another kiss – witnessed by Christina, who panicked and told Iona that Tatiana was pregnant and was planning to tell Bob after the wedding. Iona urged Bob to marry Tatiana. He did as he was told.

Tatiana broke the happy news at the reception but discovered the baby was dead. Bob blamed himself, as Tatiana already had a healthy child. She couldn't bear seeing Bob suffer and told him the truth – the baby wasn't his. Bob was devastated, but supported Tatiana as she delivered her miscarried child, before heading off to a music festival. He didn't know when he'd be back.

Blushing bridegroom Big Bob and Tatiana (Magdalena Kaleta)

Wee Bob and Stella (2012)

After a rocky start, a dodgy bit in the middle, and a visit by Stella's nasty mum, the couple finally tied the knot on Valentine's Day. Scarlett and Robbie wanted to organise the 'show' but Bob and Stella did it in secret.

Scarlett turned up on the day with some leftover grubba for Bubba and caught Bob and Deek all dressed up with somewhere to go, but they weren't telling. She then quarrelled with Frances, who had done Stella's hair, and suggested Scarlett perhaps didn't know her family as well as she thought. Deek and Gabriel acted as witnesses and the happy couple enjoyed a 'wee night' in the community centre – until shell-shocked Scarlett slapped a stunned Bob!

Valentine's sweethearts
Bob with Stella

Malcom and Liz (2012)

While Malcolm was going over his nuptials with Eileen, he referred to Liz as the mother of his children. But when he made Liz power of attorney, Eileen was furious and accused Liz of taking advantage of someone with dementia.

Gina called in on Liz and she revealed she was having second thoughts, but Gina talked her into going ahead with the ceremony in picturesque Loch Lomond. Malcolm became agitated when he saw Liz with his widow Rose's brooch – even though he'd given her it. What are you getting into, Liz?

Smiles all round. Malcolm and Liz at Loch Lomond

And then the ones that got away . . .

(2003) Cormac proposed to Jo but she didn't think he was serious and laughed.

(2005) Soppy Malcolm proposed to Shirley, but she chose grumpy George. He then proposed to Liz and she said no. Got her eventually!

(2005) Glenn proposed to Lola in The Grill but the slippery chef had no intention of marrying her.

(2008) And for Bob and Charlie, see Jimmy and Scarlett!

And that said, unfortunately, I'm afraid the marriage success rate in Shieldinch doesn't make great reading. NONE of the couples from the first SEVEN marriages have remained together, while Ruth's 2010 marriage to Andy lasted just a little longer than an episode of *River City*. But that won't deter loved-up Shieldinchers from taking the plunge in the future. Mark my words!

Disaster. Bob and Charlie didn't make it down the aisle

CHAPTER 6

Family Affairs

River City has never lacked stolen moments of passion, but forbidden trysts – now that's a different matter altogether. Schoolgirl Kirsty was banned by her dad from seeing hunky barman Russ, while Mummy was doing the dirty with nasty Lewis Cope. An awful example to set! Check out this at-a-glance guide to who was sneaking off to see a lover while the other half sat at home, and who was topping the adultery charts – like poor old Cormac, who chucked Ruth to go with her sister and was chucked three times by Jo! Serves you right, I hear you say. There has never been a dull moment in the back alleys of Montego Street, and there are no signs of the moral high ground ever winning the day – thank goodness!

FAMILY AFFAIRS

As we've seen previously, if there is one good reason for the residents of Shieldinch to get married, it's normally to indulge in an extra-marital affair. The opening episode shenanigans of Eileen Donachie and Lewis Cope set the tone for a decade of dirty deeds.

Wayward Eileen has regularly been at the heart of many moonlit trysts but even she surpassed herself by sleeping with her sister's boyfriend, Archie, while brow-beaten Gina waxed lyrical about her 'fantastic' new man. Eileen's daughter, Kirsty, even got in on the act. Like mother . . .

They say that 'fooling around' normally ends in tragedy, and it certainly did when brazen medic, Marcus McKenzie, romanced one redhead too many! And when Gina finally decided to have a little fun, her moment of passion was broadcast on Shieldinch radio!

Here are some examples of Montego Street adultery . . . and forbidden backcourt love.

In trouble. Russ Minto
(Grant Ibbs)

Eileen and Lewis (2002)

The handsome boy-made-good and his old flame, who had married Tommy ten minutes before. Eileen eventually showed Lewis the red card, but not before the fling had ruined her marriage.

Kirsty and Russ (2002)

Raymond was furious to find barman Russ Minto pulling more than pints. Kirsty, his gymslip daughter, had started seeing the handsome Russ and Raymond used some of his Shieldinch 'charm' to warn him off. Or was it a Glasgow kiss?

Cormac and Jo (2002)

Okay, so the handsome chef wasn't married when he took a shine to Jo, but he was going steady with her sister. What looked like the romance of the year was always destined to end in trouble.

Marcus and Gina/Heather (2003)

The dashing Aussie doc had a thing for redheads. Marcus raped Gina and couldn't understand why she snubbed him so moved on to Heather, which only ended when Heather killed him!

Billy and Kelly-Marie (2003)

After super-stylist Billy had slept with Kelly, she inadvertently told his wife Della that she was pregnant. Wrong. Kelly was smitten, Billy wasn't, and it turned out Billy couldn't have kids.

Lewis and Della (2004)

Okay, so it was just a kiss in the back of a taxi at first, but then Billy gambled a night of passion with his wife – and lost! Little Sammy was the result.

Eileen and Archie (2004)

Naughty Eileen was at it again, this time with sister Gina's new beau, Archie. Stolen moments of office passion spiralled out of control and perennial victim Gina was the one to get hurt, naturally.

Young Kelly, scourge of Billy Davis

Bob and Michelle (2005)

Bob finally found 'the one' after she'd given birth to a baby in the portacabin. They moved into the caravan of their dreams before scheming Michelle's boyfriend turned up and cleaned him out.

Jo and Luca (2005)

Talk about forbidden fruit. The 'siblings' were attracted to each other from the start but showed their true feelings as New Year fireworks lit up the night sky. Another relationship destined to end in heartache.

Scott and Eddie (2005)

Eddie Hunter (Derek Munn) with wife, Tina!

Montego Street's resident graphic designer had a doomed relationship with funeral director Dan but soon found happiness with DCI Eddie Hunter, until he discovered Eddie was married with kids.

Complicated. Hazel, Vader and Alanna (Jade Lezar) in The Tall Ship

Forbidden love, but Alanna and Vader were an item

Vader and Alanna (2005)

It was a fairy-tale romance. Vader, down on his luck, met Hazel, an orphan with a share in The Tall Ship. Love's young dream, until teen temptress Alanna came along and destroyed their happiness.

Charlie and Liam (2006)

Charlie was in love with Bob and their whirlwind romance included one strawberry milkshake and two straws. Then virgin Charlie decided to sleep with Liam and ruin it all. Tragic.

Robert and Moira (2006)

At least that's when it all came out in the wash. Nasty Robert told terminally ill George, his brother, that he'd had an affair with his wife Moira . . . oh, and just before you pop off, bro, Alice is my kid.

Marty and Iona (2007)

Ruth had gone all nuts at home so her caring hubby Marty looked elsewhere for some 'luvvin'. Iona was available and the pair began a sordid little affair, until Ruth found out and bopped her.

Kelly-Marie and Father Michael (2007)

Kelly and Andrew were an item until he started acting like a prat and the caring clergyman made his move. They went to Peru but fell out when it was discovered that Kelly was with (Ewan's) child.

Figment of Ruth's imagination? Marty (Daniel Schutzmann)

Archie and Niamh (2007)

Between treating his wife Gina like a doormat and trying to knock off his mum for the insurance money, Archie had time for an affair with ex-con Niamh . . . until he fell off a cliff. Or was he pushed?

Marty and Zoe (2007)

Does that man never learn? Marty called up an escort agency and couldn't believe it when Zoe turned up in a city centre wine bar. They slept together and he caught an STD.

Gina and Jack (2010)

Gina was going with Murray, and Jack was with Hayley, but the pair got it on at the radio station and broadcast their moment of passion across the 'whole' of Shieldinch. Classic.

Big Bob and Iona (2011)

Bob kissed Iona on the morning of his wedding and was caught by Tattie's daughter, Christina. She refused to tell her mum though because she wanted to keep the family unit intact. Such maturity.

Nick and Nicole (2011)

The married politician and the naughty schoolgirl. It was a recipe for disaster and that's the way it ended, with Nick's political career up in smoke and Nicole going back to her glossy mags.

Gabriel and Leyla (2012)

With Michael working at Christmas, brother Gabriel brought some festive cheer to Leyla, by kissing her. They were soon at it in the doctor's bed, and later Michael unwittingly helped Leyla change the duvet after a session with the anti-angel Gabriel.

Leyla (Maryam Hamdi) eyes Valentine's card, but is it from Michael or Gabriel?

Infidelity. Archie (Gilly Gilchrist) behind the bar at the Ship

CHAPTER 7

Montego Street Mobsters

The bad guys have been throwing their weight around again, but they always get their comeuppance in the end . . . or do they? McCabe saw off nasty J.P. Walsh but was eventually given his marching orders by Lenny's 'daughter'! In between, Lenny scared off big Graham MacLaverty – or rather, his son, Ewan, did. Lenny then played a pivotal role in his own son's death when he fell from a scaffolding rig, and he escaped the long arm of the law – again! Unfortunately Shieldinch hasn't been immune to the murkier side of life, with protection rackets, prostitution, drugs and money laundering finding a home in Montego Street.

MONTEGO STREET MOBSTERS

The *River City* bad boys are the characters we love to hate. We have willed them to magically disappear, just to give our favourites a moment's peace. Oh, how we sat and growled as Lenny Murdoch put the squeeze on 'our' wee Bob and the hard-working mechanic was forced to put in the hours to pay back the evil loan shark. And when Scarlett was living in mortal fear of bald-headed villain McCabe. Rewind to the moment when all Raymond and Roisin wanted was to run Lazy Ray's in peace and quiet, but nasty J.P. demanded a piece of the action.

But when Shieldinch is gangster-less, it shows, and producers receive letters by the sack load demanding the return of their favourite hood. Here are a few baddies who have put the menace in Montego Street.

Lenny Murdoch

Believe it or not, but it was his terrifying laugh that earned Frank Gallagher the part as evil Lenny. He was attending an audition in Dumbarton with Sandra MacIver, series producer and Paula Magee, one of two producers at that time. Frank was asked to read part of a script but when he came to a line he found hilarious, he couldn't stop laughing – which sent chills crawling down the spines of both ladies.

'You could say that was the moment Lenny Murdoch was born, although it genuinely was spontaneous laughter,' said Frank.

Four weeks later, he received a call to say the part was his, and for the unsuspecting citizens of Shieldinch, life would never be the same.

On receiving end . . . Lenny with captor, Gus

Initially, Frank was offered a three-week role, but turned it down. A few weeks later, the phone rang again and this time, he was in for keeps. And he loves his character, although not so much what he gets up to but the manner in which he can justify his actions to the one person who matters most – himself.

'Lenny is a Tony Soprano-type character,' admitted Frank. 'He cares passionately about family, and especially his grandkid – whom he loves to bits – but thinks nothing of pulling a gun on someone and blowing their head off. He's a sociopath who wouldn't dream of being unfaithful to his wife. There's really not a lot that would stop Lenny in his tracks, bar a bullet, and he's managed to dodge a few of those in his lifetime. Unfortunately for a lot of people, Lenny doesn't know the meaning of the word wrong.'

From the outset, Frank was determined to mould Lenny into the type of character he perceived him to be. He wanted to make sure his alter-ego had a sense of humour, despite the fact that every time you look at him, you're staring into the eyes of a psychopath.

'Top of the list,' said Frank, 'was to show how cold Lenny could be. How nothing but nothing fazed him. He may have been a bit of a sap in the eyes of his family, but otherwise it was business as usual and he was a ruthless man. He was just doing a job, and that's how he justified his actions.

'He had to be smarter than your average gangster, which would set him apart from other wannabe crooks. Lenny isn't a big guy in terms of height, so it was important to be sharper than the rest. Most of the Mafia aren't above 5'7", so height was never an issue.

'We had this wonderful scene with Lenny giving Father Mulvaney a lecture. There was no dialogue, just music, but you knew exactly what Lenny was saying – when the priest's face went chalk white!'

Lenny has more lives than your average moggie and this was never better illustrated than when he wrestled Shellsuit Bob into the River Clyde – a sensational and dramatic conclusion to the brilliant 'Charlie kidnap' storyline.

Frank, who was born in Coatbridge, reckoned that was the end of the bad guy and took on another acting job only to receive a call from *River City* a few months later, saying, 'We want Lenny back.'

'I was happy enough to return. I love playing Lenny and as long as you can love your character then you can enjoy it, but more than anything, I just love acting.

'Playing Lenny is the polar opposite from playing Frank Gallagher because I'm a big softie. The only problem is, though, that people think you're like that in real life!

'I did stand-up comedy for years after leaving the RSAMD, where I had "served my time" for three years.'

Frank admitted he will play Lenny Murdoch for as long as people 'enjoy' the character or producers want him. 'As long as we can keep Lenny interesting then I don't see why not. Lenny has a vital role to play in the community!'

Thomas McCabe

When McCabe first made his presence felt in Shieldinch, he had tough guy Jimmy Mullen at his side . . . and that wasn't an unusual occurrence for actor Tam Dean Burn.

Born and brought up in Edinburgh, Tam's first job was as a services department clerk for a company that maintained combined harvesters. He joined drama school at Queen Margaret in Edinburgh and served his apprenticeship backstage at Perth Theatre for a season. He said, 'Once I had started out in the acting world, that was it for me. It was 1980 and I've been doing it ever since. I thoroughly enjoy it and anyway, there comes a point when there isn't anything else you could do. I still never saw it coming though. It wasn't the career I had in mind while at school. I was more interested in punk music then!'

In 2002, and with an extensive acting portfolio behind him, Tam was invited along to the BBC to try out for the part of McCabe. 'McCabe was introduced to deal with tough guy J.P., and Jimmy was my sidekick. Billy McElhaney was someone I'd known very well for a long time. And it's funny, but in the early days of *River City*, all the gangsters were from Edinburgh. Were they trying to tell us something?'

Tam added, 'McCabe certainly evolved over the years. At first he liked the girls and had Kelly-Marie sitting on his knee, and then he appeared to favour younger girls and the likes of the girl gang. He had moved to being a type of Fagin character. Then he had a penchant for young guys and took a shine to Stevie Adams, but by that time I was confused!

'I think McCabe also saw himself as sophisticated, and I liked the way he was a real gangster with a touch of humour, unlike those in other soaps where they play it hard and are all doom and gloom.

'Near the end of my time in Shieldinch I had a lot of good and funny lines. McCabe suddenly became interested in fine art and on one occasion, when my character was late for an appointment, I said, "Sorry I'm late. I was watching the *Antiques Roadshow*."

'I'd be in someone's house, ready to give them a good going over, and would pick up an ornament and give it a valuation. It was funny.

'I enjoyed my time in *River City* and reckon most of McCabe's storylines were character-based rather than driven by plot. That shows he was a good, strong character, which was pleasing.

'It's just a pity I was killed off because I know from speaking to people that McCabe was popular, but that's life I suppose!'

Jimmy Mullen

Billy McElhaney has a couple of former *River City* colleagues to thank for bringing him to the attention of the theatre-going public, although probably one more than most. Tam Dean Burn and Kirsty Mitchell were appearing in an early Irvine Welsh play and recommended Billy to the director. The play was a smash hit, most notably because gorgeous Kirsty – who would go on to play Shieldinch honeytrap star Jodie Banks – stripped off every night, which 'crammed 'em in!'

Billy laughed. 'I reckon they also wanted to check out this young up-and-coming actor!'

Billy worked on a three-part *Taggart* with Mark McManus but it was while playing opposite Maurice Roeves in stage show *Gagarin Way* that he got the call for his first audition in Shieldinch. 'I was unsuccessful but

Reformed character . . .
Jimmy Mullen

was later invited to play the henchman sidekick of McCabe, which was fantastic because Tam and I had known each other for years.'

Billy, from Edinburgh's tough Niddrie scheme, admits he fell into acting by chance – because it was either that or mining. His dad, a miner for thirty years, insisted no son of his was heading down the pits to a life of dirt and drudgery. Billy duly took up an apprenticeship as an electrician and soon discovered that drudgery wasn't confined to 300 feet below sea level.

He explained, 'I worked as an apprentice spark in Edinburgh and had to raggle walls, etc., every single day. We had ninety-three houses to complete and it was one a day. I couldn't handle it and decided to quit.

'Tam and I ended up on the same bus one day and decided to audition for Queen Margaret Drama School for a bit of a laugh. He was a punk and I was a soul boy but we were best of mates. It was okay and we decided to stick it. I picked up a few wee parts here and there, which was a great thrill.'

Billy admits he was delighted when he landed the part of Jimmy Mullen, even though it was initially just a small role. 'It led to much bigger things,' said Billy. 'The series producer Sandra MacIver believed there was mileage in developing a relationship between Scarlett and Jimmy. I was

Murray Crozier and Jimmy on Ruth's wedding day

invited to come in for a year and have been there ever since, despite several attempts on my life!

'The Adams family are my kind of people, although I suppose they are the Mullens now. People stop me in the street and ask where Scarlett is. I just tell them she's at the bingo!' Jimmy has experienced many ups and downs during his six years in the soap, although none more devastating than being knocked down by a gang of joyriders in a stolen car. The character almost died in the accident and spent months in a wheelchair, an experience that gave him a totally different perspective on life. 'At first you're just playing a part and chuckle at not having to "hit the mark". You joke about how Jimmy would get up the stairs outside the flat but soon realise there is a far more serious side to being in a wheelchair.

Jimmy struggled in his wheelchair

'There are restrictions placed on what you can and can't do. How do you get to the toilet, up to the bar or a million and one other things? There must be a real sense of frustration and anger. Will I ever work again? Will I get the feeling back?'

Slowly but surely though, Jimmy recovered, and with a little help from Raymond and Ewan, was back walking in time for his wedding. Billy said, 'You're so vulnerable. Jimmy was once a big hard man, and then he was nothing, and at the mercy of every two-bit gangster around.'

When Jimmy lost his job, he turned to McCabe in desperation, which culminated in McCabe sticking a knife in his belly. Jimmy was left to die but thankfully Mr Mullen is made of stern stuff. 'I thought, "Is this the end for Jimmy?" Everyone has to go some time, but Billy McElhaney is happy at *River City*. You can't keep a good man down!'

Graham MacLaverty

Racketeer Graham MacLaverty reckoned there was a few quid to be made in Shieldinch but hadn't bargained on the strength of the Murdoch clan, particularly Ewan. An old crony of Lenny's, MacLaverty talked about bouncing Ewan up and down on his knee when he was just a nipper, a comment Ewan didn't take too kindly to, and he made sure the gangster got the message. He extracted a tooth from one of Big Mac's sidekicks and warned MacLaverty was next.

'That was enough for me,' joked Simon Weir, who played MacLaverty. 'I was out of there. Ewan had finally proved himself worthy of the Murdoch name.'

The part of MacLaverty was initially earmarked for an older actor, although a little tweaking meant the former *High Road* star was perfect for the role, and he looked every inch the villain in a long black coat and leather gloves. He was even giving evil Lenny a run for his money until that stern warning from Ewan.

'I had auditioned for a part five years before finally getting there. It was just a general audition, but I didn't hear back, so I was delighted when I eventually got the part of MacLaverty.'

Graham MacLaverty

Simon was opening a fashion store in London when he received the call from Shieldinch – they wanted him to start on the Monday! He said, 'It was late at night and naturally I accepted the gig, but I almost didn't make it to location on time. En route to Dumbarton, I was stopped by the police and had my car impounded for a lack of insurance. I swear I wasn't getting "into character", and made it on set with seconds to spare!

'Initially I (as MacLaverty) ran a protection racket and bullied a few girls before moving on to the Murdochs. I had been an old family friend, hence the line about knowing "baby Ewan", and reckon I could've taken him and McCabe – because I was bigger than them!

'Lenny liked MacLaverty but was wary of him because he knew MacLaverty had big ideas about running the patch. But as I was a rival of McCabe's, I could do no wrong in Lenny's eyes.'

Simon also insisted the backlot at *River City* is the best he's ever filmed on, and said, 'It's a proper film set and offers so many different options for directors. Shieldinch is twice as good as the set at *EastEnders*.'

Simon concluded, 'I'm glad MacLaverty wasn't killed off, because there's always an opportunity to go back and show Lenny who the real boss is! Okay, so there was never going to be room for Lenny AND MacLaverty in that little community but who knows what the future holds.'

Montego Street Madman,
J.P. Walsh

J.P. Walsh

Leith resident Gary McCormack had bags of experience as a tough guy before joining *River City* as frightening hood J.P. Walsh. He had won a gong for his role as Larry in Paul McGuigan's 1998 film adaptation of Irvine Welsh's *The Acid House* before working under Martin Scorsese in worldwide smash *Gangs of New York* as a member of Bill the Butcher's gang. He was also in the dramatic Norse film *Valhalla Rising*.

And when Gary's *River City* character J.P. turned up in Shieldinch and called on Roisin, she was mortified. This was one blast she was keen to leave in the past. Nasty J.P. was soon taking advantage of Roisin's fondness for Raymond and had the tanning salon boss eating from the palm of his hand. Of course, it helped that wannabe gangster Raymond fancied himself as Montego Street's answer to Jimmy Cagney!

But when J.P. started bullying Heather at Versus, she was up for sorting him out and enlisted the help of the even more sadistic Thomas McCabe (out of the frying pan and into the fire?). Of course, McCabe was only too happy to help a damsel in distress, especially when Ms Bellshaw told him J.P. was planning to skip the country – with his cash! J.P. tried to cite misunderstanding, but 'Thomas' refused to listen and told his boys to take him away. It was the end of the road for nasty J.P. but just the beginning for long-suffering Shieldinchers as McCabe took over the patch with a vengeance.

Cammy Tennant

Arguably the baddest baddie in the history of *River City* – and the only man to slash Lenny and live to tell the tale! Neil Leiper played the detested drug dealer and people trafficker, who tried to get Stevie hooked on heroin again before kidnapping schoolgirl Nicole Brodie to sell her on as a sex slave. But he met with a grizzly end when Nicole's dad Michael finally flipped and beat him to a pulp with a length of lead piping for what seemed like hours! Job done though, and Cammy expired in hospital.

Neil said, 'I'd been up for a few parts in *River City* before getting the role of Cammy – but I really couldn't have asked for anything better. It was an amazing part and yes, I do manage to sleep at night! Seriously though, when I found out what I would be doing I asked to be allowed to play the role my way. I knew exactly what was required, and I like to think I did a decent job. I know people who have become *River City* fans because of that one storyline!'

Neil, from Johnstone, Renfrewshire, first took an interest in acting when PACE Youth Theatre from Paisley visited his school to deliver a project on bullying. 'I got right into it and was invited along to join the group. I stayed for eight years and knew almost right away that acting was the career I wanted to pursue.

'*River City* gave me great exposure and I'm not really too bothered that I was killed off. Let's be honest, I don't think redemption was an option for Cammy!'

And while Cammy might never be back to darken our doorsteps, there will inevitably be other bad apples waiting round the corner. But crimes in Shieldinch are a rare occurrence, so rest easy . . . for now.

Bad lad . . . Cammy with sidekick Angie

CHAPTER 8

The Way They Were

Don't you just love raking through the old family album and giggling hysterically at Aunt Maud's changing hairstyle, or Uncle Ernie's attempts to cover up that receding hairline? Well, in ten years of *River City*, our main characters have undergone many a remarkable transformation, and lived to tell the tale. Here, we take a peek at some of the original character pics and remind ourselves exactly of the way they were!

THE WAY THEY WERE

Throughout the last ten years, the original characters have been on quite a journey, both in their personal lives and hairstyles! Gina has maintained her magnificent flame-haired locks, but perhaps they are a bit more conservative these days. Scott Wallace also managed to get through his fair share of gel in the early days, while flatmate, Ruth, initially enjoyed the cropped look. And Deek has been transformed from pre-pubescent schoolboy to dashing young entrepreneur.

Grittier. Advertising in the 'Noughties' had changed

We also tend to forget that way back at the beginning, Deek, Bob, Hazel, Brian, Kirsty and Zara were the first wave of schoolchildren, and since then we've had the Hunter brothers, Jamie and Paul, Amber, Nicki and Dilip, and now Conor and Adeeb.

Take a peek at these early pictures and decide whether or not our characters have moved on . . . for better or for worse.

River City kids. From left, Paul (Sean Brown), Jamie (Anthony Martin), Freya (Natasha Watson) and Nicki (Jayd Johnson)

Kelly's chavvy look

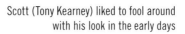

Scott (Tony Kearney) liked to fool around with his look in the early days

Ruth's crop-top look

Eileen in her 'pre-straighteners' days

Gina's 'barnet' stood out from the crowd

Deek was never without his 'battle dress'

Hazel gets ready for school

Advertising 2002 – Remember to tune in!

Bob swapped his shell suit for school uniform

CHAPTER 9

Tackling the Big Issues

Over the years, the show has tackled many important issues head on, such as HIV, ovarian cancer and miscarriage. Actors pour every last ounce of energy into making characters and storylines as believable as possible and have been rewarded with kind words from viewers. *River City*'s dedicated website now carries helpful information after sensitive storylines, and here all the biggest issues are tackled.

TACKLING THE BIG ISSUES

Compared to network soaps such as *EastEnders* and *Coronation Street*, *River City* is a relative infant, but Shieldinchers have still encountered heartache and tragedy on a scale equal in measure to the Big Two. Scottish Television's *High Road*, set in picturesque Loch Lomond, revelled in its tartan and shortbread image but still tackled many of the social issues of its day, while drawing upon a certain 'clientele' as its main viewer base. *River City*, on the other hand, is popular across a broad spectrum of society. Viewers range from the young to the old. Carter Ferguson (PC Harry Black) recalled a primary school kid offering up a memorable impersonation of Ruth Rossi one afternoon in a supermarket, while Billy McElhaney (Jimmy Mullen) remembered the time he was stopped in the street by a woman, 'Who must have been in her nineties', and asked when he was going to stand up to Scarlett!

So while the show is successfully bridging the generation gap, it has also worked hard to incorporate into the fabric of a family-based soap some of the most contentious issues of its time. Teen sex and unplanned

Award winner Paula with her BAFTA

pregnancies have formed the basis of many a storyline, as have adultery, infidelity, homosexuality and many other variations of sex. Crime too, has found a home in Shieldinch and reared its ugly head in many guises: murder, rape, assault, theft, arson, drug-dealing and fraud. Health issues have been at the beating heart of some of *River City*'s most powerful storylines, from Alice's HIV threat to Scarlett's ovarian cancer and the potential grooming of Nicole.

Almost since the beginning of her Shieldinch timeline, Ruth Rossi/Green/Carroll struggled to come to terms with mental health issues, which materialised in many different guises and had a profound effect on her family and friends.

But perhaps the most daring health issue tackled was the Down's syndrome storyline, in which Paula Sage played McCabe's tragic daughter Donna. The award-winning actress, who claimed a

BAFTA for her role in *AfterLife*, joined *River City* in 2005 and remained for the biggest part of the year. Paula was fantastic in a role which brought acclaim from the media, viewers and her *River City* co-stars. The young Cumbernauld lady was a popular cast member and continuously shared a laugh with crew and cast alike.

Tam Dean Burn, who played Donna's father, praised the BBC for tackling a subject previously viewed as taboo on the small screen. The bold but well-handled story also allowed viewers the chance to see a softer side to hard man McCabe. Tam said, 'The BBC were brave when they decided to introduce a Down's syndrome character to the show. I don't think any other soap would've dared do it.

'Paula always said it was her ambition to appear in *River City*, so that was another positive to come from it.'

Ken McQuarrie, the former Head of Programmes at BBC Scotland, said, 'As a continuing drama we never shy away from difficult issues that are appropriate to storylines but endeavour to make sure they are tackled in a sensitive way.

'As *River City* is a fictional representation of real life, we have a responsibility to properly represent the diversity of the world around us. In light of this we absolutely stand by our decision to portray a character with Down's syndrome and feel that talented actress Paula Sage played her brilliantly.

'It would be great to see more opportunities for actors with Down's syndrome and we hope that *River City* will not only have helped raise Paula's profile but also the important role of disabled characters in drama.'

Ken insisted *River City* would continue to tackle contentious issues. 'It's important for all dramas to tell stories that matter to the people who watch them. Serious issues are part of the fabric of daily life and by telling these stories we help make sense of them.

'I'm proud that we never shy away from tackling difficult subjects. That said, we also have a fair amount of light-hearted stories and humour in *River City* and it's this mix of tones that our audience often say they particularly enjoy about the show.'

Alice and Lewis (Duncan Duff) were at the centre of an HIV storm

Over the last ten years, *River City* has turned the spotlight on the thorny subject of drugs. In the early days, Rory O'Sullivan injected Lewis Cope with heroin, which spawned the powerful 'does Alice have HIV?'

storyline. Stevie Adams sold drugs from the family ice cream van, while Zoe blackmailed Dr Vinnie Shah – who was getting a bit too fond of his own medicine – for pills. The evil Archie was also buying dodgy prescription drugs to help grind down his delightful mum.

With drugs comes the inevitable bed partner of violence, and Shieldinch has witnessed its fair share of brutality – enter one Lenny Murdoch! But before the Glaswegian gangster turned Montego Street into his bespoke playground, J.P. Walsh and McCabe ruled the roost and were every bit as menacing as 'family man' Lenny.

But while viewers may frown upon Lenny's antics, many made their feelings crystal clear when he hastened his own departure from Shieldinch. Frank Gallagher, who plays Lenny, said, 'The general reaction I get from viewers is that while they despise Lenny, and the way he goes about his "business", he does make the programme more interesting, and that reaction pleases me.

'When I left, I'm told the disappearance of Lenny created a massive hole, and viewers wanted it filled. They thought the best way to do that was to get Lenny back. It seems we all love a good villain!'

Ken McQuarrie admitted that while there is no acceptable way to portray drug taking and violence, it does have a place in drama because, once again, it's a reflection of real life.

'Drug-taking, violence, etc., are part of life and we have a responsibility to portray it as truthfully as possible.

'There are no subjects or topics off-limits. It's all about how we tell the story in order to make it safe and acceptable for our pre-watershed audience. That's not to say we feel limited by what we can show before 9pm, but it can often be just as dramatically powerful to imply violence, for example, rather than explicitly displaying it on screen.'

While producers are reluctant to hail *River City* as a leader of public opinion, there's no doubt the show has done just as much as many a government campaign to get serious messages into the public domain. Scarlett's ovarian cancer scare prompted a positive response from viewers, who agreed that even though the issue

Scarlett battled ovarian cancer

had included moments of humour, it had been handled with sensitivity. The episodes in which Tatiana lost her baby saw the official *River City* website carry contact details for organisations such as the Miscarriage Association. BBC Scotland goes to great lengths to ensure that those affected by certain storylines have relevant information to hand the moment the programme has finished.

Actor Tom Urie, who plays Big Bob, was there when his on-screen girlfriend, Tatiana, lost the baby. He reckons the controversial storyline had an equally devastating effect on men as it did on women. He said, 'I received letters and messages from guys who were glad that the storyline had flagged up exactly how they felt when their partners or wives had suffered miscarriage. They were concerned that subjects like this were normally shown exclusively from a woman's perspective.

Tragic. Tatiana lost her baby

'People were asking me for advice on how to handle the situation and thankfully I was able to point them in the direction of the *River City* website. This was the first time I had ever taken on such an emotional storyline, and I was drained while shooting the episodes. It's certainly the hardest part of my job so far and I wouldn't wish it on anyone.

'I like a laugh with the crew but that stopped. The scripts were brilliantly written and Magdalena (Tatiana) and I immersed ourselves in them, but we were in a dark place and got a glimpse of how life must be permanently for people who have to go through such an ordeal.'

Ken McQuarrie added, 'We have a responsibility to engage with the issues that are important to the nation. We are dramatic entertainment first and foremost, but the powerful thing about drama is that it can explore social issues and raise awareness of them without preaching to people.

'After running the storyline about Tatiana's miscarriage, we received an email from the national director of the Miscarriage Association praising our handling of the story. It's great to get positive feedback. Working on a show like *River City* is exhausting and it's a morale boost for cast and crew to be told they're getting it right.

'Drama engages the heart as well as the head and therefore soap storylines can have a massive impact, especially when you tap into something that the audience cares about or feels affected by.'

Throughout the last ten years, *River City* has also endeavoured to reflect the increasingly diverse society in which we now live. The Malik family owning the corner shop may have appeared stereotypical, but it was the second generation of the family in which we saw a number of western influences come through. Nazir wanted to run a computer graphics store instead of following in his dad's footsteps at the shop, while Zara, the baby of the family, chose Bob as a boyfriend and skirted with her own religion by wearing the hijab.

Yet many other topics have been explored by the production team. For instance, Zoe's descent into prostitution and the sexually transmitted disease passed on to Marty. Billy Davis gambled away a night of passion with his wife to arch-enemy Lewis, which had serious ramifications for his marriage, while the abuse Alanna suffered at the hands of her foster father proved a prolonged but sensational storyline.

Zara Malik (Shabana Akhtar Bakhsh)

There are no doubt many reasons why *River City* has survived for ten years, but one of those is certainly the courage producers show in tackling the big issues head on, while doing so with respect and dignity.

And the camaraderie of the Montego Street residents often shines through. Help is at hand in times of trouble, like when Big Bob helped find Caitlin for foster parents Eileen and Raymond, or the many times we saw Scott Wallace throw a protective arm around Ruth. And who could forget the 'men' of Shieldinch standing as one to run Lenny out of town – even though they failed!

The competition for viewers is greater now than ever so these storylines are just some of the reasons why viewers tune in time and again. *River City* now has its own identity, but it hasn't happened overnight. It's not just about a bunch of characters that happen to live or work in the same street. It's a world in miniature and they have earned the right to visit our living rooms on a weekly basis – and long may that continue.

If only . . . Billy, Della and baby Sammy

Happy 'family' Ruth, Scott and baby Eilidh

CHAPTER 10

The Shieldinch Spook

Big Bob has proved popular with viewers since being introduced to the show as Molly's long-suffering son. But on his first day at work, he experienced some ghostly goings-on, and they weren't in any script! Yet this wasn't the first time The Shieldinch Spook had made itself known to cast or crew. Sound recordist Sinky had the 'pleasure' of many early-morning meetings with the spirit, and a couple of well-known characters even indulged in a spot of ghost watching! But still the sightings continued . . .

THE SHIELDINCH SPOOK

Things have been going bump in the night down Shieldinch way . . . and also during the afternoon! Several members of the *River City* team have experienced ghostly goings-on in The Tall Ship, as well as other studio sets, and many unexplained events are still, well, unexplained! Unusual noises, chairs inexplicably relocating to different parts of the studio, and a Strathclyde Police plaque spinning 360 degrees in The Tall Ship – while fixed with screws.

Ghost whisperers Gina and Stella

Tom Urie stumbled upon the Shieldinch spirit on his first day at work. He said, 'The crew were on a tea break and everyone pottered off to the canteen, but as the new guy in town, I was happy to run over my lines just outside the Adams flat. All of a sudden, I heard this voice asking, "Are you new?" I said, "Yes", but didn't know who had asked. I turned round but there was no one there.

'After I'd replied, the ghost said, "So, you can hear me," to which I answered, "Yes."

'I'm into clairvoyance but it still freaked me out, although I kept it to myself because you feel a bit daft talking about ghosts.'

Tom was then told of sound recordist Sinclair Gracie's brush with the Shieldinch spirit. 'When I heard Sinky had experienced something similar I spoke out, but apparently we're not the only people to experience it.'

BBC employee Sinclair confirmed that he had 'enjoyed' several early-morning trysts with the ghost, dating as far back as 2004. He said, 'I'm usually one of the first to arrive on location and go straight into the studio to set up the equipment for that day's filming. I quite often felt a presence and on a number of occasions, "someone" cupped my ears with their hands, although there was never anyone there.

Big Bob

'One morning I was soldering a piece of equipment next to Bob and Stella's flat and got a real fright when something put its hand on my head. There was no one there so I was out the studio like a shot!'

He added, 'It has upset a number of people on the crew, with a couple of the Art Department girls seeing strange, dark shadows lurking close by.'

But on one particular occasion, while shooting a quiet scene between Lenny and his son Ewan in The Tall Ship, an alien voice was heard over the sound crew's talkback system, and it was one which at that time was unrecognisable to Sinky.

He said, 'Lenny had just told Ewan that he was proud of him for murdering Lydia's pretend son, and that he had joined an exclusive club for murderers. Suddenly this voice said, "Oh, for f***'s sake!"'

'I screamed, "Cut" and the first assistant director came bounding over. "Why did you say that, it was a great take?" I had to tell her what had happened. We only had two live microphones in the entire studio, one for Lenny and the other for Ewan. Whatever it was had to be standing close to the actors. The assistant director was adamant no one had spoken, far less sworn, during the take.

'A camera operator spooled back the tape and there it was, clear as day, "Oh, for f***'s sake!" We all listen to the same talkback system but I was the only one to hear it.

'After that, I took off one ear of the headphones and someone kept saying, "Sinky" into my ear. It was definitely the same voice – and really spooky!'

One of the prop men also recalled the day he 'tidied up' a number of chairs used by the make-up and costume departments to view monitors while shooting studio scenes. He said, 'It was the weekend, and I arranged them in a semi-circle at the monitor but, moments later, they were all over the place again – and there was no one else in that day.

'The same thing happened at the Adams flat and again the chairs were scattered all over the kitchen set. There were also reports of strange noises in the studio, and many people believed there was definitely something in it.'

Spooked Sinclair Gracie

And there was the prop Strathclyde Police plaque in The Tall Ship bar which, rather freakily, spun 360 degrees in front of several of the crew while screwed tight to the set wall. Days later, it mysteriously disappeared!

So, next time you're watching your favourite soap, keep an eye on the background – you never know what you might spot!

CHAPTER 11

Behind the Scenes

In the following pages, we will take you on your own private tour behind closed doors at Scotland's top soap. We explore all the nooks and crannies of Montego Street and introduce you to the people behind the camera – those who help make the show the major success it is. Why are there Christmas decorations up at the start of October? Why do the gardens of Montego Street have daffodils in November? And why doesn't old Malcolm have any furniture in his house? Find out the answers to these questions, and more, in Behind the Scenes.

BEHIND THE SCENES

Dumbarton, the ancient capital of Strathclyde, is the home of fictional Shieldinch. The compound is a neat collection of old whisky and vodka bottling warehouses, with a stunning backlot thrown in for good measure. The filming hub, just a mile or so from Loch Lomond, is now home to various BBC productions, such as costume drama *Garrow's Law* and *Hope Springs*, although its primary function has always been to produce *River City*.

It's a brisk fifteen-minute walk from the nearest train station, although you could be forgiven for thinking you were nowhere near Scotland's biggest and best purpose-built media centre. Naturally, nothing advertises the studio's presence – no road signs pointing you in the direction of Montego Street, no pubs such as The Tall Ship in the vicinity.

Inside the complex, it looks as though cast and crew have simply abandoned their cars in any old place, but these are the prop vehicles, used for drive-bys and for parking up, or even to hide camera cables! In the early days, you would probably have noticed a fleet of milk floats zipping around the set, delivering bits and pieces of crew kit and props to the various sets. These have since been replaced by a small army of crew vans which double as dressing vehicles. But it's still difficult to believe that anything of great interest goes on in this area of graffiti-strewn walls and streets littered with an assortment of rubbish.

When the cameras start turning though, the set is brought to life, and that's when the backlot is at its magical best. You quite often have to stop for a reality check when you spot daffodils in the height of summer, or people walking around licking ice cream cones in February.

You then start to wonder what else on the set has lost touch with reality. Open the doors to The Tall Ship and an empty shell sits quietly where the bar should be. And Malcolm is nowhere to be seen if you push open the front door to his house. In fact, he has no furniture, apart from a scattering of dressings in his petite hallway. And the tenement blocks? Sorry, no

Tall Ship rear, scene of many a hushed conversation

one home. Pop out into the heart of Montego Street and the cast iron bollards are a mix of plastic and fibreglass, and easily moved if a camera track requires that particular space. The trees and bushes look as though they are coming along nicely, but only with a little helping hand from the art department. As the show is filmed weeks in advance of transmission, seasonal changes have to be tweaked and plastic flowers are used to great effect. And if you ever see Christmas trees and decorations brightening up Montego Street, you can be sure we're only in October!

Almost all exterior scenes on *River City* are shot on the backlot. It's far kinder on time and budget to adapt an existing space than to head out on the road with cast and crew. So, for instance, when we watched the secretive Stevie Adams–Scarlett warehouse tryst, we can be sure it was filmed in one of the adjoining, deserted warehouses.

Other buildings have been adapted to use as, for instance, hospital wards and police interview rooms. Or, in the early days, when Shellsuit Bob and Deek came face-to-face with Vader and his tough gang, the scenes were shot in the grassy area behind the subway station.

Must be October. Zoe at 'Christmas'

One advantage of filming 'in-house' is the ability to control almost everything around you, such as traffic and curious pedestrians, although some elements are still outwith your control, like aeroplanes – including one budding pilot who decided to take lessons every day for a number of weeks directly above the set – or the flock of seasonal seagulls that are particularly attracted to the rooftops and chimneys of Montego Street!

When it comes to interior scenes, the team move off the lot and into the sound-proofed studio, often a welcome haven from the wind and rain. The studio is home to sets such as The Tall Ship, Scarlett and Jimmy's living room and kitchen, and Malcolm's flat. The pub, in particular, is a strange, brightly-lit space surrounded by the darkness of the studio, in which a vast team of camera operators, make-up artists and costume assistants constantly buzz about, and it's strange being able to walk straight out of the pub and into Iona's living room!

The hub . . . the River City studio

Space is at a premium inside the studio but wherever health and safety rules allow, temporary prop stores and lighting cupboards spring up. And of course there are the areas where make-up and costume assistants sit watching monitors to make sure the actors are suitably attired and glammed-up. But however lifelike the interiors appear – and they are,

Fake beer . . . Annie Sobacz (Reanne Farley) behind the bar at the Ship

right down to the wallpaper and paint – take a closer peek at the beer pumps in The Tall Ship, for instance, and you'll find a mythical choice of Hoffman's and Doyle's Beers. But while the lager in the pump will be 100 per cent genuine, this is used merely for pouring purposes. The camera cuts and an actor will soon be drinking a (warmish) pint of non-alcoholic lager!

And take a little peek at Jimmy sitting with his drink in the corner. He is reading the *Clydeinch Enquirer*, which has just rolled off the presses in the multi-functional graphics department, which also produces fake cigarettes, passports and bus passes.

Access to sets is granted to few people outside of cast and crew, and while the public can indulge in a guided tour of the set, requests to hold private functions in The Tall Ship unfortunately have to be turned down!

But perhaps the most appropriate people to tell us exactly what goes on behind the scenes are those who know Shieldinch best. Here are just a few of the names you see on the end credits.

Jim Shields . . . Producer/Director

Jim directed the first ever episodes of *River City* and has been a constant at Shieldinch ever since, and was also at the helm when BAFTA nominations for Best Drama Series arrived in 2007 and 2009. He is also a past producer (2003–05), and said, 'I'd previously worked on *EastEnders* as a

Calling the shots . . . Jim Shields (centre) with Paul Samson (left) and first assistant Tim Bain

director so I brought that knowledge of working on an urban soap to Scotland, where few had that type of experience.

'I had enjoyed directing, and it was an honour to shoot the first episodes, but when I was offered the chance to produce, I jumped at it. It's a twenty-four/seven role though, and I found that instead of

reading a book at night to relax, I would read a script, and again with my morning coffee, and all day at work!

'Being a producer on soap is a hard shift. With other dramas, there is always a finishing line, but there is no end in sight with our genre. But it's a great job and I really did enjoy it.

'You have to know a bit of everything, from directing to scripts, and cameras to sound. But the most important aspect of the job is to remain true to an initial story idea. You must ensure it doesn't lose its way at any time during the various stages of production.'

Ron Seeth . . . Director of Photography

Ron began his Shieldinch 'stretch' in 2003 as a camera operator but a fascination for the way scenes were lit led to him learning the ropes as a Director of Photography (DOP), so much so that he is now the longest-serving DOP on the show.

Ron works alongside a team of electricians to create mood and atmosphere. He said, 'There is a description of each scene in the script. It will say, for instance, "Nighttime: Lights off, moonlight streaming through the window", and that's my licence to create that effect.

'I also ensure pictures are properly exposed. We shoot with two cameras and I watch both shots on a bank of monitors to make sure there are no shadows or booms in shot – and that no one in the background is staring straight down the camera lens!'

And while most people in the crew prefer to film in sunshine on the backlot, Ron insisted bright light can be a DOP's worst nightmare. 'It can be so inconsistent,' said Ron. 'We quite often spend an hour lighting a scene, running lines, rehearsing and then shooting it on wide and establishing shots. It's all good but when we move in for tighter shots, the sun nips behind a cloud just to spite us! It's so frustrating.

'But it's a fantastic job and we have a real family atmosphere at *River City*. You can keep Hollywood, I'm happy in Shieldinch!'

Seeing the light . . . DOP Ron Seeth

Dan Wilson . . . Director

Londoner Dan brought his directorial skills to Shieldinch after stints on *Coronation Street*, *EastEnders*, *Hollyoaks* and *Emmerdale*. But his real fear of being unable to understand the native tongue failed to materialise

Director Dan Wilson

– until he met Roisin! He said, 'Regional accents and local humour are often the main issues when moving around on the soap circuit, and *River City* has its own identity like all the others.

'In *EastEnders* you have the miserable London humour, while *Corrie* plays host to some cheeky northern chappies. Glasgow also has its own unique selling points. So, while I wasn't offered my own Shieldinch interpreter, I occasionally did have to ask my continuity lady what Roisin had just said!'

Dan, who studied Russian at university, said, 'Directing is a fantastic job but there are literally one hundred and one things you have to know. A solid understanding of film and television techniques is a pre-requisite and you need to know the script inside out, and how to transfer your vision onto the viewer's screen. In a nutshell, it's a director's responsibility to take the script and make an episode of *River City*.'

But unlike mainstream drama, soap directors are constantly battling an enemy from within – time, or rather, a lack of it. *River City* directors can be asked to produce twenty plus pages a day, which naturally places restrictions on the level of creativity a director can inject into the final edit.

Editor Ian Erskine works closely with the Director

Dan said, 'There is no better place for a director to learn his trade than on soap. You learn quickly because you have to work so fast to get through the daily shooting schedule. You have to learn all the tricks. Producers don't necessarily employ you to be over-creative because viewers just want to watch their favourite characters. If they are too aware of the hand of the filmmaker, you've overstepped the mark.

'Soap is plot and character driven rather than pretty pictures. That said, the very nature of the stunning backlot at *River City* allows far more scope to be creative and to put your own little stamp on it.'

He added, '*River City* stands shoulder to shoulder with all other soaps.

Actors such as Eileen McCallum, Gray O'Brien, Michael Nardone and Maurice Roeves could grace any production.'

Sinclair Gracie . . . Sound Recordist

To most people, the arrival of the humble seagull reminds us that spring is in the air and summer may be just around the corner. Not for sound recordist Sinclair Gracie, though. 'My job,' he explained, 'is to record and capture the best quality sound possible. I use two boom microphones, which can be held overhead or underneath, and radio mics which are hidden on the actor. Time is tight and there is a responsibility on us to get it right first time.

'And then we get the seagulls, or the "beep, beep, beep" of reversing forklift trucks. Robbie Coltrane once told the gag: "What's the difference between a sound recordist and a 737 jet? When a 737 finishes work, it stops whining."

'The actors put in a brilliant performance during a scene but background noises mean we often have to do it all again. It can be so frustrating.

'When driving to work in the morning, I check out wind directions at Glasgow Airport to see how many flights will be heading over Shieldinch that day. I'm obsessed, but I love my job and when we capture the perfect take, it's a fantastic feeling!'

Capturing sound . . . Sinclair Gracie

Stephen O'Donnell . . . Camera Operator

Stephen has been the number one camera operator at *River City* since episode one and insists that as well as having an excellent knowledge of his craft, it's imperative that operators strike up a good relationship with cast – even in the most trying circumstances.

He said, 'I remember when Sally Howitt (Scarlett) was introduced to the

Best pals Stephen O'Donnell and Sally Howitt

show and we were filming inside her ice cream van. It was tight for space and I asked her to move to the side a little. She looked at me and said, "Are you trying to say I'm fat?" It was a great ice-breaker and we've since become firm friends, which is just as well because when she gave birth to baby Madonna in the back of Jimmy's taxi, I was on the close-up!'

'The camera department has a crew of five. Two operators, two assistants and a grip, who is responsible for building tracks and operating the camera dolly, which is like a little "bogey" on wheels.' Though he was quick to add, 'We do quite a bit more than just point the camera. We offer up different shots to the director and always try to be as creative as possible.'

Crew build track for the camera dolly

And although Stephen had worked at both Scottish Television and BBC Scotland before 'settling' in Shieldinch and still manages to find the time to work on Outside Broadcasts, covering anything from football to church services, he said, 'I like to keep my hand in at different types of programming but I'm happiest at *River City.*'

Jamie McWilliam . . . Art Director

Jamie has been at *River City* since 2002. His remit covers nigh on everything we see on screen, from Archie's gold pen to the knife that killed Marcus, and baby Stuart's pram. He described his method of working like this: 'I get a script and immediately break it down, which means pulling out everything that concerns my department. This can be props, vehicles, graphics and a list of items that have to be purchased specially by our buyer. I then look to see how I can make it fresh and interesting for the viewers. Perhaps by planting brightly-coloured flowers or setting up some intricate roadworks to create something visually different.

On set. Jamie McWilliam

'Continuity is massive for us and that means liaising with the crews that filmed before us and those who follow. I've been in the business for sixteen years but every single day is different.'

Think back to drunken Alice wandering aimlessly

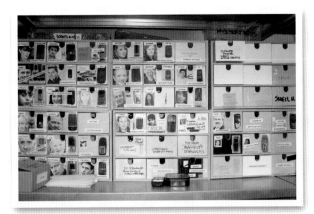

Cast mobiles

Hand props

through the boatyard, and the one constant was her half bottle of vodka, while Archie was never without his black briefcase. Little things that become a character's trademark.

Continuity and schedule might be king at *River City* but a well-organised prop store is essential. Wandering through the vast store at Dumbarton is like visiting an Aladdin's Cave, crammed full with the ordinary and the weird. Each character has his or her own section where little things such as a mobile phone, house keys and purse or wallet is kept. These plastic containers are clearly marked and stacked in such a way that they are immediately to hand.

Eileen's essential props

Items that have been produced by the show's talented graphics team, such as passport, driving licence or bank card, are retained indefinitely in case a character should make a dramatic return to the show. Kelly-Marie's personal effects, for example, would never be disposed of as she has already made more comebacks than Frank Sinatra!

Almost every small product seen on your screen is the product of the graphics team. Newspapers and the glossy magazines are all produced in-house and normally feature the names and faces of crew or production staff.

ID from the graphics team

Claire Pettifer . . . Costume Designer

Now take a walk around the costume store and marvel at row upon row of character clothing, and you'll know for sure that you've entered Shellsuit Bob zone, or happened upon Scarlett's rail. This is the work of series costume designer Claire Pettifer and her team. 'It's important that the clothing represents the status of the character,' Claire said. 'Nearly everything the characters wear comes from high street shops. There is nothing expensive or designer unless a specific storyline calls for it.'

River City isn't a glam drama, which is reflected in the costume budget,

Keeping a 'clothes' eye
on the costume store are
Dena and Karen

and Claire and her team shop wisely. 'We buy clothes where people buy their clothes, which means stores like Primark and, occasionally, Marks & Spencer.

'Sometimes we're asked for items out of the ordinary, like school uniforms or vintage wedding dresses. In fact, two of our more recent weddings, Andy and Gabriella, and Andy and Ruth, have called for bespoke wedding dresses, and we have our specialist little shops that we visit.

'The Shieldinch Stalker was a university lecturer so we gave the actor Seamus Gubbins a vintage look and picked up his outfit from a mix of charity and second-hand shops.'

One 2011 storyline had the costume assistants getting handy with a needle and thread. A group of residents decided to stage their own carnival, and staff designed a lavish outfit for hairdresser Robbie Fraser (Gary Lamont).

Claire said, 'We work to a tight schedule but when the opportunity to become creative arises, we grab it with both hands. We really enjoyed making outfits for the carnival.'

And Claire insisted that when an actor isn't too chuffed with his or her costume, they give you that 'actor look'. 'But they're quite right, because I want them to feel comfortable in what they're wearing.'

Character clothing has a shelf life and when the wardrobe store starts bursting at the seams, the team holds one of their popular costume sales. Claire explained, 'The entire cast and crew come along for a rummage and can pick up items for a few pounds. Each item comes with its own little bit of *River City* history, and the proceeds go straight back into my budget. It's a win-win situation!'

Helen McEwan . . . Make-Up

When there is just one filming crew working on the show (single banking), there are four make-up artists available for cast, while double banking (one crew filming studio, the other backlot, and shooting simultaneously) involves six. When the schedule involves a major storyline, such as a wedding, there can be up to ten artists on standby. These make-up artists are responsible for preparing characters for each scene but work within a tight schedule, with each actor allocated between twenty and thirty minutes in the 'chair'.

Helen worked as both make-up artist and designer at *River City* for six years and insisted that actors can quite often have just five minutes in make-up before being whisked

Kelly-Marie in the 'chair'

onto set by an anxious assistant director. She explained, 'Each actor has a call time and built into that is a spell in make-up and a visit to the costume department. It all works well but sometimes, for a variety of reasons, an actor is called to set early and we have to accommodate that.

'We apply a skin foundation because the base of everyone's skin tone is uneven and visible to the television camera, so our foundation gives them an even base and at least gets them out onto set where the standby artists can apply the finishing touches. We then get a minute or two at "final checks" just before shooting the scene for real, to make sure actors are good to go.'

Tear sticks are used when crying is required, although Helen much prefers it if actors can make themselves cry naturally. She said, 'Tear sticks are great, but can redden the eyes and take a while to clear. If an actor is required in the studio for a completely different storyline it can cause problems.

'Most actors can make themselves cry. Gray O'Brien and Allison McKenzie were particularly good, although they had lots of practice, with so many emotional scenes!

'Quite often, this type of scene will be scheduled at the end of the day to prevent continuity problems. Time is of the essence on soap.'

Helen loves nothing better than a good fight, which gives her an opportunity to put into practice skills learned during her apprenticeship. And like all other aspects of television production, tricks of the trade are vital.

She said, 'We can't stop in the middle of a fight to apply blood, so the actor (who loses) will have a tiny blood capsule in his mouth and bite on

Final checks. Zinnie Hassoun (Nalini Chetty) has some last minute make-up applied

it just as he is thumped. We also have little dishes of blood hidden on the set which actors can dip into, as long as they're out of vision.

'If a character has a scar or swelling, we have a lotion which can be moulded onto the skin and then coloured. We can use certain paint to match bruising and cuts.'

Helen added, 'Hair and make-up can tell a story. When Ruth was going through troubled times we slowly stripped back her make-up. Morag was always perfect but we initially took off her eye shadow and then some of the colour from her face until she was completely "naked", and that helped achieve the look of a broken woman.

'Being a make-up artist on *River City* can be challenging, as you often have to think on your feet, but it's a great job and one that I thoroughly enjoyed.'

The make-up department are the experts when it comes to transforming actors into characters, but there was another type of transformation taking place down Shieldinch way, and there wasn't a bit of blusher in sight!

PC Harry Black never solved a crime

Carter Ferguson . . . On-Set Fight Coordinator and Actor

Carter isn't proud of the fact that in 142 episodes of *River City*, his alter ego, PC Harry Black, failed to solve a single crime. As the actor himself points out, even *Balamory's* fictional bobby PC Plum's record is somewhat more impressive – because he rescued a cat!

Harry definitely wasn't on the take, due to his 'good-cop, good-cop' tag – although he did get the girl! His protracted romance with Ruth was must-see television. He said, 'Long before I was in *River City* I was an ardent fan because mates such as Sally Howitt (Scarlett) and Tam Dean Burn (McCabe) were involved.'

And there's more. Carter has been responsible for most of the grappling and hair-pulling in Shieldinch, although not literally. He is a trained fight director and spends hours off camera making sure Gina Rossi and Scarlett are 'getting it right', or that Gabriel and Leo Brodie aren't hurting each other too much while scrapping over Jo.

But far from buckling under the weight of arranging his own fights with Ruth during her 'psychotic' episodes, Carter thrived on the dual

Carter Ferguson in action mode on set

role. He said, 'I was in a privileged position. Lots of people would've given their eyetooth to be where I was, and still am to a certain degree – although maybe not when Ruth was being difficult,' he chuckled.

The Bellshill actor was initially interested in art and design but got a real kick from a small part in the school production of *Guys and Dolls*. 'After that I enrolled at the Scottish Youth Theatre where I studied stage craft and etiquette, and was fortunate enough to learn fight-arranging from Bert Bracewell, a former Olympic fencing coach.'

But surprisingly, Carter landed his first TV part in *Taggart* – playing the drums! 'I couldn't play a note,' he admitted. 'And when they shouted, "Cut" I couldn't hear and continued to play for another twenty seconds!' Other roles followed, but a theme kicked in. He played a cop in *High Road*, *Complicity* and *Tinseltown* before landing the role as PC Harry Black. Oh, and he's since played a policeman in the David Tennant drama *Single Father*, in between arranging fights for the former Doctor Who! 'I suppose if you look like a cop that's what you'll get.'

But it was playing alongside Ruth that brought the amiable actor to the attention of a soap-hungry public. He said, 'Initially I was brought in to *River City* to direct a fight between Gina and Scarlett. It was a classic catfight in Scarlett's backcourt. It was great stuff.'

Carter was then asked to audition for the part of the Shieldinch Strangler but was unsuccessful. 'Soon after, I landed the part of Harry, whose first job was to arrest Ruth when she threw her mum down the stairs, so the die was cast!'

There are a few things Carter would've changed about his character. 'The name,' he laughed. 'I don't think I look like a Harry – and the fact I never solved a crime. But most of my storylines involved some great actors, with Morag right up there with the best. I also played alongside Frank Gallagher (Lenny), Michael Nardone (DCI Whiteside) and Derek Munn (Eddie Hunter). That was the golden time for me.'

But even though Harry has left Shieldinch, Carter is still in the thick of the action, putting that fight training to good use.

The Word is Out

Hapless Harry isn't the only one with a story to tell, however. Spare a thought for the poor scriptwriting department who must come up with over fifty hours each year of top-notch plots; the equivalent of flying to Australia and back. In story terms, it's an enormous amount of material for the writing pool to find and lots of characters to develop and keep interesting. There are around thirty principal characters in Shieldinch and it's up to the bank of scriptwriters to ensure they each get their fair share of the action.

For one hour-long show, writers must come up with three main storylines, as well as many small 'beats', or elements that move the story forward, for secondary stories. Martin Brocklebank has been writing for

Martin Brocklebank, scriptwriter

River City since 2002 and also has experience of *EastEnders* and *Doctors*. He said, 'The purpose of the "beat" is to remind the audience what's going on with other characters. In the past we've had up to five or six stories running in an episode, although that doesn't happen so much now.'

The writing team regularly get together to discuss both potential short- and long-term storylines and the result of such discussions forms the basis of what we see on our screens. It would be at such a meeting that the decision would be taken to kill off a central character such as pub landlord Tommy Donachie or Ewan Murdoch, whereas if an actor decides they want to leave, producers and writers would discuss the best way in which to deal with their departure.

Martin added, 'We have to be able to write for each character in a believable way. For example, Deek is very different to Bob, Gina to Eileen, and Michael very different to Gabriel. If you get the characters right then you get the show right.'

Once a decision is taken on which storylines to proceed with, these are developed over a period of time before being worked into a script and distributed to a core writer, who will then breathe life into the characters involved and the situation they find themselves in.

Writers work well in advance but the exact term varies. There can be as much as six months between the writer receiving the commission and the episode being transmitted.

So what comes first, story or character?

'That's the age-old question,' insisted Martin. 'The chicken or the egg. I think in any long-running drama series STORY tends to have the upper hand, just because new story ideas are the "fuel" of the show and without them the show would grind to a halt.

'But characters must act in a consistent way if they're to remain believable. The audience wouldn't buy it if one of our regulars started behaving completely out of character (unless there was a legitimate, dramatic reason for him/her to do so). I think characters in long-running shows perhaps need to be more flexible than in other dramas.'

In 2010, we were introduced to the Brodie family, a throwback to day one when clans were the cornerstone of Montego Street and the bulk of the action centred on the actions of the Hendersons or Maliks. 'I think the Brodie family has been one of the biggest *River City* success stories

of the last few years. Families offer lots of opportunities for conflict, and that's why soaps are usually built around strong family units, but it's not always guaranteed that introducing a family en masse will work. Much of that is down to casting, and I think the Brodies were cast very well. There are great dynamics between all the actors in the family. I really enjoy writing scenes between Michael and Nicole, Michael and Gabriel, Leyla and the kids, and so on.'

Brothers Leo and Michael Brodie in surgery

And Martin also described the introduction of young Callum Adams as a masterstroke. Lenny has been the bane of Scarlett's life since he first brought his scowling face to Montego Street. But now, through Callum, the families are united. Well, almost.

Martin said, 'When I first found out about the storyline, I thought it was a great idea. Lenny and Scarlett have always been fantastic arch-enemies so to throw them together through a shared grandchild is inspired!'

One of the most controversial decisions in ten years of *River City* was the move from two half-hour weekly slots to a single, one-hour episode. The decision met with mixed reaction and led to several adjustments

New arrivals, the Brodie family

in the way departments functioned, but none more so than the script department.

'As a writer,' Martin said, 'it was a big change. I'd been writing the show as a half-hour soap since the beginning, so moving to one-hour was quite a challenge. For starters, you have to write more words! (A one-hour *River City* script can be around 14,000–15,000 words.) But more than that, you have to think about the pace and structure of the episode differently, you have to start thinking and writing more "continuing drama".

'On the flip side, the longer slot allows you to delve deeper into stories and characters and explore darker, more complex needs and motivations, which is great.'

Deek

One way in which a writer's life can be made more 'comfortable' is if an actor is cast before the writing process begins. This means a face and a voice to put words to, rather than starting off with a blank sheet of paper. 'That's a big bonus, even in terms of being able to see a new character in your head,' Martin added.

But Martin insisted that writing out someone they have come to love can be tough. 'I remember writing scenes when Kelly-Marie was leaving for the first time and I was gutted, not only because I love her as a character, but because I know how strong the bond is between her and Scarlett and how bad it was going to be for her mum.'

Naturally, scriptwriters have their favourites, and Martin loves writing for Deek. He said, 'I had to write the scene where he confronted his horrid dad in front of the whole community and told him to leave. The tragedy was that Deek had been waiting all his life to meet his dad and now here he was, telling him to get out of town. I cried when I wrote that scene.

'But it's great to be able to write for such a wide range of characters, although I can't help but feel a certain attachment to some of the originals, such as Gina, Eileen, Raymond, Deek and Bob. Scarlett and Jimmy are also two of my favourites, just like Lenny, Big Bob and Stella'.

Martin added, 'I was asked to write both the 500th episode and also the fifth birthday storylines, which was a great honour. In the 500th episode, Robert took Nicki and Shirley hostage. Maurice Roeves (Robert) wrote to me afterwards to say how much he'd enjoyed the story, which is the only time an actor has ever thanked me for writing a part for him!'

Unspoken Roles

But there is one group of artistes whom scriptwriters can gloss over while penning episode after episode of *River City* . . . although these 'characters without words' are an important cog on the wheel. Ricky Gervais brought the genre into the public consciousness with his hilarious sit-com but, to be honest, television and film simply could not function without them. They are our highly-valued extras, or to give them their correct twenty-first century moniker 'supporting artistes' (SAs). They breathe life into the background of both exterior and interior scenes, in sets such as pubs, shops or doctors' waiting rooms.

Of course, the BBC 2 show *Extras* hammed up the subject matter, with Gervais playing Andy, the jobbing extra with big aspirations, while Ashley Jensen was superb as hapless Maggie, a girl with ideas above her station. It worked well and was no doubt responsible for an upsurge in applications to join agencies such as GBM, run by occasional Tall Ship barman Graeme Miller.

Graeme, who was made redundant by computer giant IBM, was introduced to the industry by a friend not long after *River City* started. He said, 'We would take our instructions from the third assistant director and listen or watch out for cues, which are normally visual. Our instruction could be as simple as standing at the bus stop or stopping to chat to someone in the street.

Graeme Miller

'I loved it and tried to get as much television work as I could. *River City* seemed a great place to work and the cast and crew were friendly. Not long after, I was looking to start my own business and hit on the idea of a casting agency. I did my research and spoke to many people to make sure I wasn't getting into something I couldn't handle. I set about recruiting people who were reliable, punctual and with a great aptitude for set etiquette, which is so important because while on set they are representing my agency.'

Set etiquette requires SAs to have an understanding of how their role fits in with the way the television industry operates. This can include miming only during a scene or refraining from staring down the lens of a camera. Oh, and making sure your mobile is switched off at all times!

Extras can bring Montego Street to life. While viewers concentrate on, perhaps, a conversation between Michael and Leyla as they walk home from the surgery, it's important for the background to look real. Imagine how fake and apocalyptic it would look if no one else were around. Or The Tall Ship with no customers! While filming in the Ship, the director will rehearse the scene with principal cast only before deciding on how many extras should populate the background. This is governed by time.

Extras singing their hearts out

If the pub has just opened, one or two drinkers only. Call in on a Friday night at 9pm though and it will be heaving. Drinkers galore, someone playing the fruit machine and SAs bustling to and from the loo!

Graeme played a supplementary barman at the Ship for five years, although nowadays it tends to be a cast member, such as Charlie or Zinnie, pulling the pints. Graeme said, 'I enjoyed the experience enormously and, my "character name" was Graeme, to keep things simple. I would either be serving customers or "wiping" shot. This means, simply, walking directly in front of the camera lens to perhaps collect empties or perform another task.

'I've had a number of speaking parts, although nothing outrageous, just a simple, "There's your change" or "Hi there."

'Good extras have a vital role to play. I've watched programmes where the extra looks as if he or she has literally been pushed into the movement in a very robotic way. If I'm noticing that, others are too. But extra work can be anything but regular or glamorous and quite often SAs have to wait around in the wind and rain for their cue. In saying that, I have 200 folk on my books and they all seem happy to take the work when it comes along. Whether that be enjoying a cuppa in the Oyster or picking up another extra in a taxi, they all play their part in making *River City* the great success that it is.'

It'll be All Right on the Night

Lewis Cope: nasty piece of work

River City is a well-oiled machine, but occasionally things go wrong . . . like the time Moira Henderson tried to serve up some grub at the opening of Gina's night-time café. Of course, it was anything but all right on opening night! It was packed to the rafters and Moira made a rather unusual entrance. Holding four plates of top-notch chuck, she breezed through from the back kitchen – and went straight up in the air! All eyes focused on poor old Duncan Duff (Lewis Cope), who was closest to the actress as she made her entrance, but he was breathing easier when a rogue cable was outed as the trip hazard.

Actor Jo Cameron Brown who plays Moira suffered a painful elbow injury but the 'show must go on' and she was up in a flash and soon armed with four more pieces of the Oyster's finest bone china. However, a couple of days later, she was back in the café serving up teas and coffees to an army of thirsty Shieldinchers. Pride of place goes to the retro cappuccino machine, but the gadget had been left on and pumped out a gush of piping hot steam just as Jo started to prepare a customer's latte. The result was an unfortunate scalding and once again Ms Cameron Brown was off to see the first aid officer. So, imagine our horror when the veteran actor was 'killed' in a car crash soon after by her troubled grandson, Brian (William Ruane). If there is indeed a God, it makes you wonder why the poor woman was put through the horrors of the previous few days!

Brian certainly had lots of anger inside, especially when his mum's infidelity threatened to break up the family home. After she'd slept with Lewis, Brian rushed over to Mr Cope's portacabin with the intention of smashing it up. Picture the scene . . . he sneaks into the yard, finds a crowbar lying on the ground and heads inside to trash the joint. Okay, cut! Right, William, let's switch the crowbar to the fake rubber one. It's there for a reason. Nope? Okay, but be careful. *Doing*! He smashes the steel crowbar off a wooden desk and up it comes and smashes him straight on the forehead. Nurse! Off he went to hospital for a couple of stitches . . . and a bruised ego.

Brian Henderson
(William Ruane)

William was a good lad and provided us with bags of entertainment, especially when one of his prized rats, named Roisin after the receptionist at Lazy Ray's, ran up his leg and nibbled his bits. It happened during Brian's 'dark' spell and while he was holding Hazel hostage in the basement of the derelict kiltmaker's shop. His only friends were the little four-legged furry creatures, but even they decided needs must! Thankfully, for William, this particular incident took place off camera.

It must have been a Henderson thing, because even though Shirley was a lady with her feet planted firmly on the ground . . . that all changed when prop man George came along! At Shirley's house, the kitchen was the regular hub of activity, with gallons of tea consumed. The fourth kitchen wall was fitted with hinges to allow it to swing in and out and give a camera operator the space to catch a shot of the front door opening. On one occasion, Shirley was poised to open the door to George's nasty brother, Robert, and had a camera positioned directly behind her. *Rata-tat-tat* went the door and up she jumped. She had only moved a pace or two when the director roared, 'CUT!' She made to sit back down but by that time, ever-efficient George had whipped away the chair to allow the cameraman in. Oops, Shirley hit the deck and red-faced George looked horrified. After some hastily-provided medical treatment (TLC), filming was able to continue.

Fall. Shirley Henderson

More Hendersons . . . and one of the big early storylines surrounded the mystery of Alice, Deek's mum, and daughter of George and Moira. By way of explaining her long-term absence, writers had Alice living somewhere in Europe. On the morning of Deek's birthday, a parcel arrived, which George signed for. He handed it over to the unwitting schoolboy, who ripped it open. Deek grumbled, 'Why would I want a Kilmarnock strip, I don't even support them!' Trouble is, the present was quite clearly a Juventus strip, and they play in vertical black and white stripes, unlike Kilmarnock, who wear blue and white. One quick visit to the producer and the line was changed to a 'Dunfermline' strip!

But back to the Oyster Café, a set in which the art director and prop man have the opportunity to put their creative stamp on the show – and one prop man certainly left his mark on Gina Rossi! Shellsuit Bob and his girlfriend, Charlie, were sharing a romantic moment. Gina was to deliver two chocolate milkshakes and was wearing a rather fetching brightly-coloured blouse. The first assistant director called for calm as the crew prepared to shoot the scene. The prop man moved in to froth up the milkshakes. Wrong! Never switch on your cappuccino stirrer before plonking it in the glass. The result was Gina's brightly-coloured blouse turned a rather embarrassing shade of brown, and the glitch held up filming while the costume department set about delicately cleaning and drying the blouse. We'd already seen Gina wearing the blouse in a previous scene and continuity is God in soap! Once Gina's blouse, and the prop man's face, had returned to normal colour, they were able to shoot the scene and everyone had a good laugh.

Back to Shellsuit Bob and a different storyline. In a coma in hospital, with family and friends fretting for Scotland, and there's still time to wind Mr Purdon up. Stephen is a big Rangers fan in real life, and John Murtagh thought it would be a good idea if scriptwriters made Shellsuit Bob a Celtic fan. So, in a bid to help bring him back from unconsciousness, the prop man draped a Celtic scarf over the headboard of his hospital bed and there wasn't a thing he could do about it – he was in a coma after all! Payback time for Mr Murtagh, though, as the script team had decided the Henderson clan should be RANGERS fans.

And finally . . . Amber (Lorna Anderson) once had to dash from the hall into the living room with some exciting news for her family. She was wearing high heels and managed just fine during rehearsals. Action! Lorna ran down the stairs, turned the corner into the living room and suddenly disappeared from the monitors. The director called, 'Cut!' and the crew burst out laughing because Lorna had slipped and fallen on her bum. But they weren't alone, as tears streamed down the cheeks of Lenny and Lydia, Amber's mum and dad.

Now, where would the 'caring' crew get material for their prized Christmas out-takes tape if it wasn't for the occasional mishap? But these are few and far between, although as you can see they provide cast and crew (and now you) with some light-hearted moments along the way.

Adamses all glammed up

CHAPTER 12

Did You Know?

Learn the tricks of the television trade and find out which two *River City* songbirds came within an octave of representing the United Kingdom in the Eurovision Song Contest. Were The Tall Ship and Oyster Cafés really supposed to be called something completely different? Who is the official *River City* giant and why do Montego Street residents turn their nose up at Gina's 'tasty' ice cream? And we reveal the sisters who should in fact have had a younger brother to dote on, but whom we have never set eyes on. It's all here, in the next couple of pages.

DID YOU KNOW?

*R*iver City diehards are well aware that Amber's Hola boutique was previously Wok My World AND the old kiltmaker's, and that Bob and Stella live at No. 5 Montego Street – but did you know that . . .

Unthinkable. The 'Central' Café model

. . . the Oyster Café's original name was the Central Café and that the Maliks' corner shop was initially to be called Akram's, the original choice of name for the show's first Asian family

. . . horror of horrors, but The Tall Ship was originally to be known as The Anchor Inn

. . . Gina Rossi, alias Libby McArthur, was in the Eighties girl band Sophisticated Boom Boom. The Glasgow trio recorded a couple of shows for legendary Radio 1 DJ John Peel's Sessions

. . . the whisky served in The Tall Ship is watered down Coca-Cola. Cold tea was used previously, as was a substance called burnt sugar, but diluted Cola is now the choice of prop men, most notably for its quickness in making

. . . the ice cream served up in the Oyster Café is actually Philadelphia cheese – because normal ice cream would melt in the heat. Imagine it with a flake on!

Old name The Anchor Inn

. . . in the early years, Jason Pitt was the tallest member of cast and crew! During down time, actors and crew would stand against a studio structure to discover *River City*'s official giant! The brooding chef measured up at 6'4"

. . . twins were used for the scenes involving Ruth's baby Eilidh. Strict rules govern the use of minors on set and this allowed more time to film the many scheduled baby scenes

. . . Carmen Pieraccini's first acting role was as a boy in *The Lion, The Witch and The Wardrobe*. She played Edmund because she had short hair and there was a shortage of young male actors!

. . . Eileen and Gina had a younger brother, Robbie, who was supposed to be living in Manchester in 2002

Opposite top: Gina and Eileen . . . but where's Robbie?

Opposite bottom: Mirage. Shona at Paisley Sheriff Court

. . . Laura McMonagle and Jayd Johnson (who played the Cullen sisters Zoe and Nicki) are best friends in real life

. . . when Shona was arrested and tried for bigamy, the graphics department superimposed Paisley Sheriff Court behind a snap of actress

Julie Duncanson and superimposed footballer Andy Murray onto a packed European football ground. The photographs were actually taken in a public park in Dumbarton

. . . the staff canteen at Dumbarton has doubled as a prison visiting room and hospital ward

. . . songbirds Laura McMonagle and Jade Lezar (Alanna) were in the running to represent the UK at the Eurovision Song Contest in 2006

. . . a former *River City* director, Brian Horsburgh, allowed the production to use his photograph to double as Gina's late husband Franco

. . . when Ewan Murdoch (Chris Brazier) was rehearsing his final scenes, he almost slipped and fell from the 100ft scaffolding rig. For the actual filming, he changed his boots, used a harness and thankfully an experienced stuntman was there to take his leap of death

. . . Tom Urie (Big Bob) is related to Jackie Onassis and former US President John F. Kennedy

. . . Deirdre Davis (Eileen) was born in Liverpool and didn't move north to Glasgow until she was three

. . . Gary McCormack (J.P. Walsh) was strum-thing special before joining the soap. He was a member of high-profile Scottish punk band The Exploited, between 1980 and '83, and played bass guitar on albums *Punk's Not Dead* and *Troops of Tomorrow*

. . . Alice and Lewis were scripted to head to New York for the weekend but the budget didn't stretch that far, so the art department superimposed pics of the happy couple onto generic pics of the Big Apple – and Alice wore a New York t-shirt!

. . . James Young is the only actor to have played two different parts in *River City*. He was Reagan, leader of the gang who terrorised Zara Malik, before playing Kelvin, boyfriend of Michelle and dad of Rochelle, who 'relieved' wee Bob of his caravan contents

. . . Johnny Beattie (Malcolm Hamilton) is celebrating sixty years in showbiz this year. Just half-a-century ahead of your favourite soap!

Opposite: Songbirds Jade Lezar and Laura McMonagle

Alice and Lewis in 'New York'

CHAPTER 13

The River City Soapbox

We think it's high time our loyal viewers were given the opportunity to tell us what they think about *River City*, so the next couple of pages are dedicated to YOUR thoughts on the last ten years of events in Montego Street.

THE RIVER CITY SOAPBOX

Over 750,000 people tuned in to the opening episodes in September 2002 and while that figure dropped dramatically in the ensuing months, around half-a-million now regularly look in as the trials and tribulations of Shieldinchers are played out in our homes. Here, a cross-section of viewers explain why they wouldn't dream of missing a single episode.

'I've been watching *River City* since the very beginning and I think it has great storylines, brilliant cast and characters, and a good mix of local humour and dialect. I never miss an episode! I've toured the set several times and have also been to the BBC at Pacific Quay to research Shieldinch events. I've also made some great friends through the programme. Happy 10th Anniversary, *River City*, here's to another ten years and beyond for my favourite programme! For me, it just keeps on getting better.' – Nicola Bowers, Greenock

'Enjoyed visiting the *River City* set immensely. Been watching the show since 2007.' – Joe Gardner, Glasgow

Wee Bob and Deek

'Love it all and have watched since it started!' – Doreen Rose

'Been watching since 2006 and liked when Archie Buchanan and his mother used to live at their old house with Gina, but Archie was nasty!' – Ross Kerr

'I have been a fan since it started and love wee Bob. The show is ace and I love how they tell the stories.' – Karen Todd

'Watched from the start and have simply loved the journey!' – Joann Clark

'I didn't take to *River City* straight away but kept with it and it soon improved. There have been many great episodes such as Gina and Archie, and also when Molly came into the show, but my favourite episode has to be big Boab and Tattie losing the baby. It was so emotional. Many great characters but my favourites are Molly and the two Bobs. Keep up the good work.' – Sandra Clark

Evil Archie Buchanan
(Gilly Gilchrist)

And all the way from the US of A… 'I stumbled across *River City* in October 2010 and knew I'd be back each week. While Amber's infatuation with that perennial deadbeat, Fraser, at times drove me to near madness, ultimately she did the right thing on every level by pulling the trigger on McCabe and taking responsibility for that action. Raymond is outstanding as the landlord of The Tall Ship.

'I applaud *River City*'s decision to address ovarian cancer, down to shining light on the common misconception that breast cancer is the greatest scourge of women. Although it is highly atypical for any patient to survive ovarian cancer, Scarlett's experience was well-written and not beyond the pale.

'Still, what first led me to *River City* was the knowledge that it was about Glasgow, with actual Scottish actors, speaking with their natural r's, l's, and full vowels intact. I love when Stella or Scarlett open up wi' a whurr o' pure Lallans.' – Richard Mires, USA

'A friend of mine is eighty-four and hasn't missed an episode since it began.

Molly

Retro Amber outside new look Hola

I go up to do her hair regularly and we enjoy a wee catch-up and a blether about the characters. My son also loves it, and he's just nine.' – Tracy Symington

Ruth outside The Tall Ship

'Can't believe it's ten years since *River City* first graced our screens. I remember talking about this new show set in Glasgow and watched the very first episode, unsure of how it would portray Glasgow life. And sure it had a shaky start, but like the city itself it grew till it became the much-loved part of people's lives that it is today. There are few shows where the characters feel like family, friends and even enemies for that matter. I feel I can really connect with or relate to them and that's what makes it more than just "any soap".' – Sharon Dougan

'Watched the programme since the start and it's now better than ever. Fave character is Stevie. No matter how hard he tries, temptation will always be there. People should give him a chance.' – Jennifer Rodger, Dunblane

'Have watched *River City* from the start and never miss a week. My daughter is fourteen and watches it with me.' – Mary Maxwell

Gathered round the table

'I love *River City* and have watched it from the start. It's the highlight of my week, and I just luv the Glesga patter!' – Yvonne Keenan

'My mum, dad and sister had been fans for years and I used to berate them for watching "a lot of rubbish" – until a year ago when my sister was over and it was on in the background. I started watching it and haven't missed an episode since. The actors are brilliant, the script amazing and I love the fact that each week you get a complete story from start to finish. I now berate myself for missing so many episodes.' – Irene Gault

'I watched the clairvoyant episode alongside kids I work with and everyone in the pub was amazed at how the woman could know about Malcolm's wife and Scarlett's criminal family. The kids sat open-mouthed until one fifteen-year-old turned to me and said, "She's good, isn't she?" Of course, all the other kids started laughing. Me? As a childcare professional, I kept a straight face! We later found out that Lenny had prompted the "clairvoyant" and the girl said to the rest of the kids, "Ah, yous knew that already, didn't you?"' – Donald Nelson, Glasgow

And finally, being an avid fan myself and having worked on or watched every episode of *River City*, I've decided to include my five favourite storylines. But there have been so many great plots and stories that choosing 'just five' proved an incredibly tough task. What to leave out became the main issue.

'Cal's Kidnap' made it into the five because for once Lenny Murdoch was shown at his most vulnerable (although it didn't last long!). It was sad, though, that his relationship with Frances suffered as a result.

'Scarlett's Cancer Scare' was played out with such realism, and a tremendous sensitivity, that actor Sally Howitt was regularly lauded for her performances by the viewing public – and it kept us on the edge of our seats.

When Jimmy Mullen was knocked down by reckless joyriders, we willed him to overcome his dreadful plight and show the courage needed to battle back from such a terrible illness – while also trying to sort out his 'women trouble'.

For many years, nasty McCabe had been despised by the Shieldinch community, but when he came face-to-face with arch-rival Lenny in the infamous amusement arcade showdown, one of them was set to bite the dust. What an inspired twist-in-the-tale though, when it was revealed that the lovely Amber had gunned down the feared hood – and is now serving time in prison as a result!

But, for me, the pick of the bunch has to be the kidnap and intended grooming of none-the-wiser Nicole. Add her underage affair with Stevie Burns, himself battling heroin addiction, her step-mum's affair with Nicole's uncle, a dad who appears to have little time for his family, and the evil Cammy Tennant, and we had a momentous couple of months wondering how it would all pan out. Just brilliant.

Do you agree with my choices?

The Author's Top 5 Storylines
1 – Nicole Goes Missing/Michael's Subsequent Arrest (2012)
2 – McCabe Shot in Arcade/Amber Arrested (2011)
3 – Jimmy Knocked Down by Joyriders/Jimmy's Paralysis (2007)
4 – Scarlett's Cancer Scare (2010)
5 – Cal's Kidnap/Evil Agnes (2012)

'Watched the programme since the start and it's now better than ever. Fave character is Stevie. No matter how hard he tries, temptation will always be there. People should give him a chance.' – Jennifer Rodger, Dunblane

CHAPTER 14

RIVER CITY: The Future

The final chapter where we turn our sights on the future of Scotland's greatest soap. Even though it may be the end of the book, it doesn't mean it's the end of the show! Long may it continue!

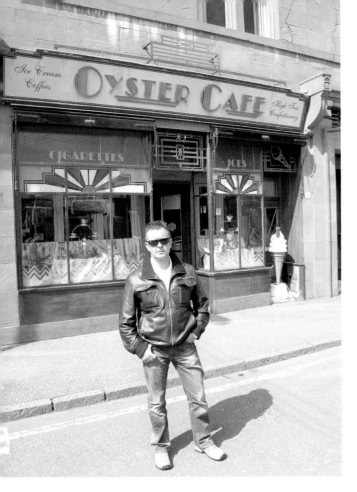

Executive Producer
Graeme Gordon

RIVER CITY: THE FUTURE

We're almost at the end of our ten-year tour of Shieldinch and, boy, have there been some terrific memories. But what next – another fantastic decade, or even longer? *Coronation Street* and *EastEnders* have clocked up many successful years and there is absolutely no reason why *River City* cannot follow in their footsteps.

Executive Producer Graeme Gordon has been in Shieldinch for almost three years and in that time, he has made a number of changes, both subtle and major. He was initially series producer before being promoted to executive producer – that means the buck stops outside his office door – but he wouldn't have it any other way. He was the driving force behind the dark and edgy Nicole kidnap storyline, which covered abduction, prostitution, people trafficking and murder. Quite a collection, and the grizzly plot wasn't confined to Shieldinch's murky underbelly. Dr Brodie's family were at the centre of the madness and he, ultimately, cast the final stone by bludgeoning bad guy Cammy to death. So was there ever a moment when Graeme felt he might have crossed the line with that particular storyline? 'Every minute of every day,' he said. 'But from the moment I was made up to exec. producer, my goal was to keep the show fresh and, yes, edgy, if you like.

'But the whole Nicole kidnap business did wonders for our viewing figures. The Audience Index figures are the ones that matter, and they were through the roof. They also tell us how much an audience liked a particular show, and the feedback was phenomenal.

'I want to make *River City* the best I can for people. I won't hesitate to change things in the future if it keeps the show fresh and interesting.'

Michael Brodie (Andy Clark) and
wife, Leyla (Maryam Hamdi)

Graeme insisted that the 'show' in question is no longer a soap. 'It's hard to describe it that way when it's once a week and an hour long. *River City* is definitely a drama.'

Background music now has a massive part to play and the accompanying piece to Michael's brutal assault on Cammy, 'Sacrifice' by Lisa Gerrard and Pieter Bourke, was the most requested piece of music in BBC Scotland's recent history. 'I like music in the programme,' Graeme said, 'but it must earn its keep and help tell the story, and that particular piece, I felt, did its job well. We spend a lot of time going through the BBC's music library to make sure the music is just right.

Jo disrupts the Heart of Glasgow ceremony

'I think *River City* has a bright future. It's often difficult delivering fifty-two hours of programming each year on a tight budget, but we do the best we can and, by all accounts, the show is very well received. We try to keep an open mind and see what we could be doing better, because it's important that *River City* continues to evolve.'

And so say all of us. The last ten years have flown by and I, for one, can't wait for the upcoming plots, whether they be gritty, witty or just about plain old Shieldinch life. We've covered the characters, stories, loves and losses of residents and given you a sneaky peek behind the scenes. We haven't lauded the saints nor judged the sinners – that's up to you, the viewer.

Sisters at war . . . Ruth and Jo

For me, the show is now going in the right direction, and that's onwards and upwards. We don't just have words telling the stories anymore, but also an unforgettable soundtrack that adds so much to the product.

Those of you – and there are many – who have signed up for the ride are the lucky ones. Those yet to sample the delights of Montego Street are in for a real treat. Thanks for joining me on this amazing journey, and see you in 2022!

(Shellsuit) Bob Adams (Stephen Purdon) 2002–

Not the best of upbringings, what with a jailbird dad and rent-a-mouth mum, but Bob has a heart of gold. Gutted when he found out his mammy wasn't really his mammy! Been in: *Ratcatcher*.

Kelly-Marie Adams (Carmen Pieraccini) 2003–

Nice but dim Kelly has left for Monaco and Peru but always returns to her beloved Shieldinch, although the last time she came back, she brought a wee bambino! Been in: *Dear Green Place*.

Paddy Adams (Gilbert Martin) 2003–2004

Scarlett's man was a wrong 'un. Turned up after being released from jail and proceeded to annoy the life out of everyone. Knocked her about a bit and gave his kids a hard time.

Stella Adams (Keira Lucchesi) 2009–

Sleeping rough when Good Samaritan Deek decided he wanted to help because she reminded him of his mum. Then he asked her out – dodgy! Married Bob on Valentine's Day . . . aaah!

Stevie Adams (Cas Harkins) 2003–2005

The flying postie dropped into Shieldinch when Bob was in a coma and romanced Hazel and Scott! Caught up in a drugs scandal with McCabe and ended up in the pokey.

Ajay (Roshan Rohatgi) 2005

Financial trader turned actor introduced to sort out Cormac when he started seeing Alisha. Tried to carve up the big chef but Zak stepped in to prevent Cormac's kitchen nightmare.

Ally (Marcus Nash) 2011

Leader of the gang who bullied schoolgirl Nicole Brodie. Pick on someone your own size!

Bob Adams (Stephen Purdon)

Ajay (Roshan Rohatgi)

Sammi Amari (Samia Rida) 2008–2009

Ben had just proposed to Sammi when he was knocked down and killed by Ewan, who later hit on an unsuspecting Sammi. She chased him when he eventually confessed.

Angela (Alana Hood) 2007

High-class call girl who worked out of Lazy Ray's along with Lena. Shellsuit Bob was besotted with her.

Jodie Banks (Kirsty Mitchell) 2008

The attractive cop fell in love with nasty DCI Whiteside – then busted him as soon as he confessed to a bundle of crimes.

Spider Barclay (Paul Donnelly) 2009

Turned up in Shieldinch looking for Jimmy's dad, Kid, who owed him money, but Jimmy sent him packing. The Kid then short-changed Spider before speeding off in Jimmy's taxi.

Heather Bellshaw (Jenni Keenan Green) 2003–2008

Estate agent Heather was introduced as a tonic for Raymond's ailing love life, but turned Blinc Inc. into Versus wine bar, then murdered Marcus before heading for Oz. Been in: *Single Father.*

PC Harry Black (Carter Ferguson) 2004–2008

Ruth sent Harry to hell and back. He took charge of the heist at the docks but was cut up, metaphorically speaking, when fellow cop Eddie Hunter was killed.

Charlie Bowie (Ryan Smith) 2009–

The university student and budding author had the unrivalled distinction of being dumped three times by Annie – in the same episode!

Jennifer Bowie (Lorna Craig) 2009

Charlie's sister caused a stir when she tried to kiss best pal Amber. Was the life and soul of the party but left Shieldinch to travel.

Alanna McVey (Jade Lezar)　　　　　　　　Alice Henderson (Lorraine McIntosh)

Alisha Shah (Meneka Das)

Andy Murray (Sam Heughan)

Adeeb Brodie (Taryam Boyd) 2010–

Struggled to settle in Scotland and wanted to go back to Iraq. Hooked up with step-brother Conor and discovered the vagaries of alcohol. Fell through the dodgy portacabin floor.

Conor Brodie (Rian John Gordon) 2010–

Ran away with his Uncle Leo to the loch but Leo tried to commit suicide. He helped him come to terms with his problems and ultimately saved his life. A big fan of Burns!

Gabriel Brodie (Garry Sweeney) 2010–

Opened an amusement arcade, much to the disgust of locals, and slept with Jo, his brother's gal. Christmas kiss with Leyla shocked the nation!

Leo Brodie (Nick Rhys) 2010–2011

The troubled soldier struggled to deal with life after Afghanistan and tried to commit suicide. Ploughed his compo into the amusement arcade but left Shieldinch with Jo and Romeo.

Leyla Brodie (Maryam Hamdi) 2010–

Widowed at a young age and married the 2010 version of grumpy George Henderson, Dr Brodie. Nicole's rock, until she was caught snogging Gabe.

Dr Michael Brodie (Andy Clark) 2010–

Head of the Brodie brood and always too busy to spend time with his family. Moans a lot at his wife, brothers, kids and just about everyone else. Apart from that, he's really a nice guy. Stepped up to the plate when he dispensed with his 'charms' to eradicate Cammy! Been in: *The Da Vinci Code*.

Nicole Brodie (Holly Jack) 2010–

Scheming little madam who caused the marriage break up of politician Nick Morrison. Slept with Stevie while underage, then was kidnapped by evil Cammy. Phew!

Callum Stuart (Donald Pirie)

Carly Fraser (Michelle O'Brien)

Arun Shah (Ricky Dhillon)

Billy Davis (Gray O'Brien)

Archie Buchanan, aka Douglas (Gilly Gilchrist) 2004–2010

Evil personified. Why any man could want to harm poor Gina and Eileen – especially when he's married to one, and the other's his mum – is beyond comprehension. Been in: *Crossroads*.

Stevie Burns (Paul James Corrigan) 2011–

Ex-drug dealer Stevie was determined to go straight and found 'love' with fifteen-year-old Nicole, although he was arrested for underage sex and had to leave Shieldinch.

Andy Carroll (Jamie Michie) 2009–2011

Fell for Ruth while at school but she broke his heart – twice. True love has a way of righting life's wrongs though, and they re-united. Occasionally though, Cupid gets it wrong.

Sheila Carroll (Alison Peebles) 2010

Nasty piece of work who tried to prevent her son marrying Ruth. Hang on – maybe she's a good mother after all.

Liam Cave (Paul Hickey) 2003

The Shieldinch Strangler turned up in Montego Street and butchered Tommy Donachie while holding Kirsty Henderson hostage. Presumably still supping porridge.

Chris (Dean Anthony Fagan) 2010

Community centre worker who enjoyed winding Deek up but helped him when Deek's flat was broken into.

Lewis Cope (Duncan Duff) 2002–2005

Mr Nasty survived a 'heroin hit' by Rory O'Sullivan to become public enemy number one in Shieldinch. Conquests included Eileen, Alice, Della, etc. Been in: *Burke and Hare*.

DC Will Cooper (Scott Ryan Vickers) 2012–

Robbie's love interest and DCI Donald's understudy. Poor guy! On the trail of nasty Sean.

Charlie Drummond (June Brogan)

Cormac O'Sullivan (Jason Pitt)

Deek Henderson (Gordon McCorkell)

Della Davis (Katie McEwan)

Niamh Corrigan (Frances Healy) 2006–2007
Ex-lawyer did time for bad guy Archie and when released from prison, discovered he was still a cad. Like most Shieldinch women, though, gave him another chance and paid the price.

Morna Cowan (Claire Dargo) 2010
Ex-jailbird pal of Theresa's who turned up demanding cash owed by her former cellmate. Turned her lackeys on wee Bob but Theresa got it instead. That was allowed.

Fraser Crozier (Neil McNulty) 2010–2011
Lad with ideas above his station. Did well with Heavenly Herbals and bagged a trophy date in the shape of Amber. Should've quit while ahead but tried to fleece Lenny. Silly boy.

Murray Crozier (Brian Cowan) 2010–
Soft-touch Murray wooed Gina but she had a brief fling with Jack because Murray wasn't exciting enough. He took her back, though, and they fell out again!

Nicki Cullen (Jayd Johnson) 2004–2010
Turned up looking for her big sister Zoe and her waster mum, Patricia, and went through the whole gamut of teenage emotions. Targeted by evil Robert and Mac the child predator. Been in: *The Field of Blood*.

Patricia Cullen (Caroline Paterson) 2004
Staggered out of a taxi after a drunken one-night stand (for cash) and straight into her disgusted daughter, Zoe. Stuck around for a bit before doing us all a favour and slipping away.

Zoe Cullen (Laura McMonagle) 2004–2008
Girl gang leader who blackmailed Dr Vinnie Shah into giving her drugs, which she sold. Then became a valued member of the community before turning to prostitution. Been in: *Ae Fond Kiss*.

Dr Marcus McKenzie (Stefan Dennis)

Duncan Robertson (Kieron Elliot)

Dilip Shah (Aron Sidhu)

Donna McCabe (Paula Sage)

Dan the Undertaker (Deepak Verma) 2003

Scott Wallace had a near-death experience when he slept with Dan! The undertaker was soon cheating on Scott, who chased him out of town – naked! Been in: *EastEnders*.

Billy Davis (Gray O'Brien) 2003–2007

Constantly in trouble with wife Della due to his infidelity, especially with Kelly. When Della left he had a series of ill-fated affairs with Jo, Tina and Scarlett. Been in: *Coronation Street*.

Della Davis (Katie McEwan) 2003–2005, 2007

Billy's long-suffering wife turned a blind eye to his 'fooling around' for years but longed for his babies. Gave birth to Sammy after a one-night stand with shady Lewis Cope.

Hazel Donachie (Annmarie Fulton) 2002–2006

Tommy's daughter eventually found happiness when she married Vader. Didn't last long though and she eventually left to travel round the world (with Vader). Been in: *Sweet Sixteen*.

Tommy Donachie (Eric Barlow) 2002–2003

Mine host at The Tall Ship but first out the door when he was murdered by the Shieldinch Strangler. Married to Eileen but you have to wonder if the marriage was ever consummated! Been in: *Orphans*.

DI Donald (Robin Laing) 2011–

Pressed Frances for info on Lenny and warned her that he would investigate her mum if she didn't. Only vocation in life was to nail Lenny . . . oh, and sleep with Frances (Vivien).

Eddie Hunter (Derek Munn)

Eileen Hamilton (Deirdre Davis)

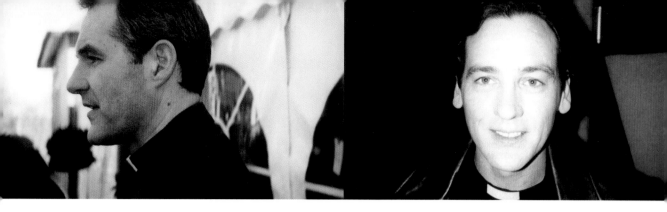

Father Dominic (Peter Vollebregt)

Father Michael (David Murray)

Drew (Daniel Healy) 2010

Member of The Bobtones with Big Bob and Iona. The geeky kid had grown into a talented, hunky guitarist and Iona melted when she saw him. Jealous Bob chased him.

Charlie Drummond (June Brogan) 2006–2008

Introduced as a cleaner in Versus and fell for Bob instantly. They got engaged but she was kidnapped by Lenny Murdoch. Slept with Liam and then jilted Bob at the altar.

Jean Drummond (Kate Donnelly) 2008

Bob's annoying, overbearing mother-in-law, until she sided with the wee man and advised him to ditch her daughter.

Father Dominic (Peter Vollebregt) 2006–2007

Father Michael's religious 'interest'. Mostly told Michael what he should and shouldn't do, even though Michael never listened. All the time, dodgy Dominic had his eye on Eileen.

Father Michael (David Murray) 2005–2007

As deep as the spiritual ocean one minute, Versus drunk the next. Thumped scummy Andrew's mate after he insulted Kelly. Moved to Peru with Kelly and that was that.

Father Mulvaney (Laurie Ventry) 2010

Advised Ewan Murdoch to do the right thing and clype on his dad, but Lenny found out and threatened him in the confession box.

Ben Franklin (John P. Arnold) 2008

Shieldinch stint was short-lived, as moments after he'd proposed to girlfriend Sammi, he was mown down by a tired Ewan Murdoch.

Carly Fraser (Michelle O'Brien) 2005–2008

Arrived in Shieldinch as a member of the girl gang and took naked pics of Deek at a wedding reception! Ran Carly's Café.

Freya Robertson (Natasha Watson)

George Henderson (John Murtagh)

Fi Kydd (Monica Gibb)

Frank McKenna (Jon Morrison)

Lily Fraser (Ida Schuster) 2002–2003

The outspoken OAP was the perfect foil for Malcolm but made one too many visits to her son in Canada and the Adams family nicked her house.

Lola Fraser (Suzanne Bonnar) 2005

Single parent who landed a job at the Deli. She was duped into believing Glenn loved her. Some you lose, others you also lose!

Gabriella (Shelley Lang) 2010

Set to marry Andy until Ruth produced her 'Mrs Robinson' moment and halted the wedding. Pretended she was pregnant but Andy didn't buy that old chestnut.

Helen Gilmore (Gerda Stevenson) 2003

Ewan's partner caused quite a splash when she arrived in town. The unhinged broad pretended she was with child, stole Jo's then jumped in the River Clyde (not with the kid!).

Marty Green (Daniel Schutzmann) 2005–2008

Husband of crazed Ruth. Their relationship was compulsive viewing, as was his deceitful on–off affair with Iona. Ended up with syphilis through sleeping with escorts. Been in: *Footballers' Wives*.

Eileen Hamilton (Deirdre Davis) 2002–

Opted for a career in the local council before becoming a mum for the third time. The tables turned when Gina eventually stood up to her.

Gina Hamilton (Libby McArthur) 2002–

Cornerstone of *River City* but the lowest point of her ten-year tenure was undoubtedly the rape storyline. Tried murdering second husband Archie but didn't do a very good job. Been in: *Looking After JoJo*.

Gerry McGrade (John Paul McGilvary)

Gina Hamilton (Libby McArthur)

Glenn McAllister (John Macauley)

Graham MacDonald (Gordon Kennedy)

Liz Hamilton (Eileen McCallum) 2005–
Looked down her nose at daughter-in-law Gina when she first arrived, calling her 'beefy', but has since managed to cull her incessant snobbery somewhat. Poisoned by her evil son. Married Malcolm in 2012. Been in: *The Steamie*.

Malcolm Hamilton (Johnny Beattie) 2002–
Patriarch of Shieldinch and owner of doos! The widower was romantically linked with Lily and Shirley, although had to wait until Liz came along before he got some decent company – and a wife!

Zinnie Hassoun (Nalini Chetty) 2011–
The ultimate minx. Liked nothing better than causing trouble but exceeded herself when she grassed up Stevie to the police when he nicked Gina's flat keys.

Alice Henderson (Lorraine McIntosh) 2002–2008
Left for London when she was just sixteen – after having Deek. Came back for his sixteenth birthday, which was thoughtful. Died in a road traffic accident in 2010. Been in: *Hope Springs*.

Brian Henderson (William Ruane) 2002–03, 2009
Product of a broken home and when his stepdad Tommy was killed, took an unhealthy shine to Hazel. Killed his gran in a stolen car and was locked up for kidnapping Hazel. Been in: *The Wind that Shakes the Barley*.

Derek Henderson (Gordon McCorkell) 2002–2012
Brought up by his grandparents until his mum arrived back on the scene for his sixteenth birthday. Entrepreneur but unlucky in love. Been in: *Jeopardy*.

Jamie Hunter (Anthony Martin)

Jamilah Malik (Laxmi Kathuria)

Hazel Donachie (Annmarie Fulton)

Heather Bellshaw (Jenni Keenan Green)

George Henderson (John Murtagh) 2002–2007

Was a racist, sexist, bad father, husband and general grump. Paid his daughter to leave town when she gave birth at sixteen then found out Alice wasn't his child. What a waste of money! Been in: *Braveheart*.

Kirsty Henderson (Kari Corbett) 2002–2003

After having a step-sister foisted upon her she did everything in her power to muck up Hazel's life. Became a goth and ran away to Wales, where she died in a car crash. Been in: *Monarch of the Glen*.

Moira Henderson (Jo Cameron Brown) 2002–2004

Turned out this devoted wife and mum had affairs with her brother-in-law and daughter's son's dad! Eventually killed in a car being driven by her grandson Brian.

Raymond Henderson (Paul Samson) 2002–

Jack the Lad who owned Lazy Ray's and The Tall Ship. Divorced Eileen, wooed the gorgeous Heather and married Roisin, and her sister Shona – twice!

Robert Henderson (Maurice Roeves) 2007

Turned up when his brother George was dying and took over from Ruth as the show's resident psycho. Vandalised George's bench before taking Shirley and Nicki hostage. Phew! Been in: *Bookie*.

Shirley Henderson (Barbara Rafferty) 2004–2009

Della's mum swapped Spain for Shieldinch (crazy lady) and plumped for grumpy George over Malcolm (crazy lady). Part owner of Moda Vida. Been in: *Rab C. Nesbitt*.

Jimmy Mullen (Billy McElhaney)

Joanne Rossi (Allison McKenzie)

Karim Malik (Kriss Dosanjh)

Kelly-Marie Adams (Carmen Pieraccini)

Lee Hope (James Palmer) 2010

Started out as Lydia's pretend son, courtesy of Lenny, and turned into a psychotic, jealous and dangerous young man. Maybe he WAS Lenny's son!

Dr Dan Hunter (Adam Robertson) 2011–

The new practice doctor was a recovering alcoholic with a gambling habit! Gambled away a fortune using the practice credit card. Stood up to Lenny, though. Respect!

Eddie Hunter (Derek Munn) 2004–2007

Got a wee bit too close to nailing Lenny and paid price. The gay cop was getting on well with boyfriend Scott – till Scott's wife and kids showed up in Shieldinch. Oh, and someone shot him!

Jamie Hunter (Anthony Martin) 2005–2008

The most stable Hunter – until he was caught stealing bras and stalking Iona. His inclusion on the sex offender's register proved the catalyst for the fractured family's move to Mull.

Paul Hunter (Sean Brown) 2005–2008

Suffered most from his dad's decision to 'come out' and turned to arson to gain attention. Almost killed old Malcolm when he set fire to his lock-up. Thumped his mum.

Tina Hunter (Jenny Ryan) 2005–2008

God knows how Tina didn't end up in an institution with that lot for a family. All she ever wanted was a bit of happiness, but it was too much to ask for apparently.

Joe (Sean Scanlan) 2009

Ex-pro who helped out at the community centre as a boxing coach but hid his fondness for the bottle until Marianne caught him sipping the amber nectar.

Lewis Cope (Duncan Duff)

Liam McNulty (Patrick Mulvey)

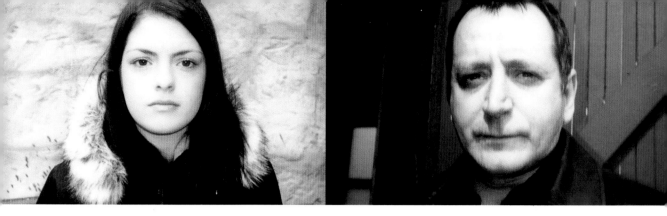

Kirsty Henderson (Kari Corbett)

Lenny Murdoch (Frank Gallagher)

Hamish Johnston (Stewart Preston) 2010–
Lenny's lawyer who did all he could to help Amber get off with her murder charge. Has spent a lifetime in cop shops with Lenny.

Alex Judd (Brian McCardie) 2009
Bent councillor went up against Eileen in the election – and lost. That was the end of his career in politics, and backhanders from Lenny.

Frances Keener (Andrea Hart) 2011–2012
Mysterious woman who turned up at McCabe's funeral and instantly tried to seduce Lenny – although not at the funeral. That would've been just wrong! McCabe's sister.

Sean Kennedy (James Cunningham) 2012
Anyone who isn't frightened of Lenny is either stark raving mad or the toughest guy in the world. Nasty Sean is a bit of both. Lowest of the low.

Lena Krausky (Anna Kerth) 2007
One-half of Shieldinch's resident call-girl duo. Lena rented Lazy Ray's to use as a seedy massage parlour but offered more than just a rub for muscular pain.

Fi Kydd (Monica Gibb) 2006–2008
Ex-sheriff who sent down Alice for downloading child porn, then Alice decided she fancied her. Befriended Shirley but met a grizzly end when she realised Douglas was really Archie. Been in: *Two Thousand Acres of Skye*.

Michael Learmonth (Seamus Gubbins) 2009
The Shieldinch Stalker attacked Ruth and Gina then lured Scarlett to his den of iniquity under the pretence of teaching her how to understand the classics. Great chat-up line.

Lily Fraser (Ida Schuster)

Liz Hamilton (Eileen McCallum)

Lola Fraser (Suzanne Bonnar)

Luca Rossi (Juan Pablo di Pace)

Sandy MacKinnon (Robert Cavanah) 2011

Annie's abusive ex turned up in Shieldinch and started a fling with Eileen before reverting to type and trying to get inside Annie's head again. Run out of town.

Glenn McAllister (John Macauley) 2005

Involvement was short and sweet. Cormac's old jailbird mate got a job at The Grill as a chef and led fiancée Lola in a merry dance, promising her the earth and delivering just the crust.

Agnes McCabe (Kay Gallie) 2011–2012

McCabe's evil mum was hell-bent on avenging her son's death. Turned up in Shieldinch (care home) with her daughter, and ally, Frances. Devil woman.

Donna McCabe (Paula Sage) 2005

Found in the street by Gina and Scarlett and taken in by the latter. Daughter of gangland hardman McCabe. Involved in several big storylines before going off to live with dad.

Thomas McCabe (Tam Dean Burn) 2004–2011

The ultimate gangster. Steely eyes spooked every resident of Shieldinch. When former sidekick, Jimmy, betrayed him, he stabbed him. Shot and killed by Amber.

Hayley McCrone (Pamela Byrne) 2009–2012

Resident crimper and just the gal to keep idealistic Robbie in his place. Despite three years in Shieldinch, never quite found 'the one'.

Graham MacDonald (Gordon Kennedy) 2004–2005

Deek's dad turned up in Shieldinch not long after his mum returned from a sixteen-year hiatus. But he was a nasty piece of work with a penchant for young girls. Been in: *Red Cap*.

Moira Henderson (Jo Cameron Brown)

Niamh Corrigan (Frances Healy)

Malcom Hamilton (Johnny Beattie)

Marty Green (Daniel Schutzmann)

Gerry McGrade (John Paul McGilvary) 2004–2008

The shady lawyer was caught up in a few dodgy dealings but came up trumps when he 'snared' Heather. Blotted his copybook by taking drugs and eventually suffered a major stroke.

Stuart McGregor (Iain de Caestecker) 2009

Roared into town in a souped-up car and caught Nicki's eye. Eventually took up boxing – and went off with Amber!

Iona McIntyre (Claire Knight) 2006–2012

The brilliant Iona wooed half the show's male characters on her first day – including Scott! Slept with Shona's man when she was just sixteen and had a fling with Marty.

Roisin McIntyre (Joyce Falconer) 2002–2007

'Rosie', as wee Bob called her, became a cult favourite. Won the lottery, married Raymond, went out with Sonny and discovered the daughter she'd given up at birth.

Shona McIntyre (Julie Duncanson) 2006–2008

Man-eating Shona (must've been a McIntyre trait) was already hitched when she married doting Raymond and a bigamy trial ensued. Integral part of anti-burger protest.

Daniel McKee (Ewan Stewart) 2008–2009

Ten years in jail taught Daniel a few lessons and he put his time inside to good use by teaching Shieldinch youngsters how to box! Responsible for opening up The Base.

Marianne McKee (Frances Grey) 2008–2009

Prison psychiatrist initially counselled Daniel, and ended up marrying him. Sparred with Daniel's young charges while he was away on business!

Frank McKenna (Jon Morrison) 2004

McCabe's lawyer and right-hand man. Devised the cunning plan that saw Heather get off – literally – with murder.

Nicki Cullen (Jayd Johnson)

Paul Hunter (Sean Brown)

PC Harry Black (Carter Ferguson)

Raymond Henderson (Paul Samson)

Dr Marcus McKenzie (Stefan Dennis) 2003

Ex-*Neighbours* star caused quite a stir when he swapped Erinsborough for Shieldinch. He saved baby Franco, raped Gina and was murdered by Jo. Talk about an impact signing.

Steph McKenzie (Emma Campbell Webster) 2003

Troubled daughter of nasty Marcus arrived with boyfriend Callum to avenge the death of her dad. Knifed Jo after the High Court trial with the weapon that killed wicked Marcus.

Sharon McLaren (Sarah McCardie) 2008–2009

Bonkers Sharon was daft the right way. She wooed Raymond then stole every last penny of his savings. Turned up a wee while later to try and win him back but he had her arrested.

Liam McNulty (Patrick Mulvey) 2006–2008

Troubled Liam snared a job as chef in The Tall Ship on the recommendation of sponsor, Father Dominic. He then snared Charlie, Alanna and Eileen.

Alanna McVey (Jade Lezar) 2004–2006

Arrived in Shieldinch to visit mum Roisin, who had given her up for adoption just after she was born. Turned out she had been abused as a child by her 'dad'.

Alex McVey (John McGlynn) 2005

Alanna's horrible step-dad who had been abusing her for years. Tracked her down to Shieldinch but died when he inadvertently blew up the caravan. Been in: *The Queen*.

Janet McVey (Aline Mowat) 2005

Loved Alanna as a daughter and dumped her husband as soon as she found out about the abuse. Been in: *The Bill*.

Ruth Rossi (Morag Calder)

Scarlett Adams (Sally Howitt)

Roisin McIntyre (Joyce Falconer)

Russ Minto (Grant Ibbs)

Innes Maitland (Sam Robertson) 2009–2010

Innes and Charlie moved into George and Shirley's flat and 'christened' it with a big hair party. Innes took up boxing but discovered he had epilepsy and left to go and stay with Beth.

Hana Malik (Mamta Kash) 2002–2003

Arch-enemy of Scarlett until her daughter Zara started 'courting' Shellsuit Bob. The warring ladies called a truce to break up the young lovebirds.

Jamilah Malik (Laxmi Kathuria) 2002–2003

Hit on Scott Wallace at a party and was shocked when the young man informed her that he was gay.

Karim Malik (Kriss Dosanjh) 2002–2003

Shop owner wasn't too happy when his son, Nazir, told him he didn't want to work in the store. Was also married to Shazia, which Hana wasn't too happy about.

Nazir Malik (Riz Abassi) 2002–2003

Love interest of Jo Rossi and partner in the computer graphic business, Blinc Inc., with Scott. Died in a car crash.

Shazia Malik (Sharon Maharaj) 2004–2005

She fancied Heather and tried to kiss her, which Heather didn't take too kindly to. Fiddled money out of trusting Roisin at the Deli and made her getaway – on the subway!

Zara Malik (Shabana Akhtar Bakhsh) 2002–2003

Dated Bob – remember the cherry picker? – and helped him out of his coma before leaving to study at Aberdeen University.

Christina Michalka (Caitlin Gillespie) 2011–

Settled with her mum and Big Bob but when she saw him kiss Iona on his wedding day, she kept it secret. When he left, she tracked him down to Helensburgh.

Scott Wallace (Tony Kearney)

Shazia Malik (Sharon Maharaj)

Shirley Henderson (Barbara Rafferty)

Shona McIntyre (Julie Duncanson)

Tatiana Michalka (Magdalena Kaleta) 2011–

'Tattie' was Big Bob's 'first love' but had several skeletons in the closet, namely a hubby, bun in the oven, a lover etc., etc. Tragedy struck when she lost her baby.

Russ Minto (Grant Ibbs) 2002–2003

The Tall Ship barman stepped straight into Raymond's bad books when he hooked up with schoolgirl Kirsty. Stayed at the student flat with Ruth, Jo and Scott.

Nick Morrison (Colin McCredie) 2011

Breezed into Shieldinch as an election candidate but soon became the object of young Nicole's desires and promptly left town after WINNING the election! Been in: *Taggart*.

Hannah Morrison (Frances Thorburn) 2011

Nick's missus did all she could to help hubby win the election but after 'Nicole-gate' she dumped him!

Kid Mullen (Tam White) 2009

Jimmy's dad was a good-for-nothing shyster who left Shieldinch almost as quickly as he arrived.

Jimmy Mullen (Billy McElhaney) 2004–

Gangster sidekick of McCabe was tasked with keeping an eye on Scarlett for the ace face. He did more than that. Had a baby with her but was left paralysed after being knocked down.

Madonna Mullen (Sienna Glackin) 2006–

Introduced to the world in the back of her daddy's taxi and the apple of Scarlett and Jimmy's eye.

Scarlett Mullen (Sally Howitt) 2003–

Arrived in the standard she's accustomed to – a tacky ice cream van – and immediately noised up the neighbours. Battled ovarian cancer and had Madonna on Christmas day. Been in: *Trial & Retribution*.

Thomas McCabe (Tam Dean Burn)

Tina Hunter (Jenny Ryan)

Steph McKenzie (Emma Campbell Webster)

Stevie Adams (Cas Harkins)

Jake Munro (Russell Barr) 2007

Salsa teacher took on a residency in the Ship, but Raymond hired him for a private lesson in how to move those hips, with hilarious consequences.

Sonny Munro (Angus MacInnes) 2008

Roisin's Yankee boyfriend decided to open Sonny Burgers when he moved to Shieldinch but hadn't reckoned on the feistiness of the Montego Street women. Been in: *Eyes Wide Shut*.

Amber Murdoch (Lorna Anderson) 2007–2011

Grew up fast. Shocked to discover her best buddy Jen fancied her, and was distraught when big brother Ewan was killed. Disowned her mum and dad and shot McCabe.

Ewan Murdoch (Chris Brazier) 2007–2010

Shieldinch hunk only wanted to make his dad happy. All turned sour when he fell to a terrible death, but left a legacy in the shape of baby Callum.

Lenny Murdoch (Frank Gallagher) 2005–

The baddest man in town. Muscled into McCabe's patch then brought his dysfunctional family to live in Shieldinch. Developed MS, and shacked up with McCabe's sister.

Lydia Murdoch (Jacqueline Leonard) 2007–2011

Gangster's moll who opened up Hola boutique, which prompted a hilarious one-woman protest by Scarlett. Stuck by Lenny until he ripped the family apart. Been in: *EastEnders*.

Rory Murdoch (David Paisley) 2007–2009

Lenny's son struggled with his sexuality and eventually ran away with a barman from Versus.

Vader (Ryan Fletcher)

Dr Vinnie Shah (Archie Lal)

Zak (Zak Hanif) 2005

Zara Malik (Shabana Akhtar Bakhsh)

Andrew Murray (Sam Heughan) 2005–2006

Whisked Kelly off to Monaco after he signed for the French League side but his ego got in the way of their relationship and Kelly chose Shieldinch.

Bob O'Hara (Tom Urie) 2009–

Introduced as a Santa Claus on the run from the police. The downtrodden son of Molly suffered anguish when Tatiana lost the baby. On/off with Iona was class TV. Been in: *Still Game*.

Molly O'Hara (Una McLean) 2010–

Nasty piece of work but compulsive viewing – to see how she could possibly eclipse previous shameful acts. Never won mum of the year, surprisingly enough!

Theresa O'Hara (Maureen Carr) 2010–2011

The biological mum of Shellsuit Bob left him with Scarlett when she was jailed, then did her best to break her sis. Thankfully she failed.

Cormac O'Sullivan (Jason Pitt) 2002–2005

Psycho chef showed a softer side when he fell for Ruth, then her sister Jo! Fell in love with Della, because he thought she was having his baby, but it was Lewis Cope's . . . aargh!

Rory O'Sullivan (Steve Ramsden) 2003

Heroin addict brother of Cormac returned to Shieldinch to settle an old score with family rival Lewis Cope.

Jack Paterson (John Comerford) 2010–2011

The hairdresser had a love–hate relationship with his boss, Gordon. Embarked on a dangerous liaison with Hayley, which was met with great disdain from Gordon, who turned out to be her dad.

The Registrar (Raymond Mearns) 2011

Officiated at the wedding of Big Bob and Tatiana.

Viv Roberts (Louise Jameson) 2007–2008

Introduced as a pal for Shirley and to give her a shake, and boy did it work. Viv wanted to party like it was 1999. Swore by internet dating but left to look for her long-lost son. Been in: *Tenko*.

Duncan Robertson (Kieron Elliot) 2005–2007

Ex-hubby of Heather turned up with the cute little daughter she'd conveniently forgotten all about! Had a life-threatening illness, which, thankfully, was cured. Caring folk, scriptwriters!

Zoe Cullen (Laura McMonagle)

Freya Robertson (Natasha Watson) 2005–2007

Heather's loveable daughter turned up with her dad and tugged at her mum's less than maternal heartstrings. Cute face soon melted the Versus owner.

Sally Ross (Tracey Robertson) 2004

Social worker had the nightmare job of sorting out who was worse – Jo or Ruth!

Franco Rossi, Junior (Romi Singh, Jamie Blyth) 2003–2008

Nazir and Jo's son was born in a close and eventually brought up by Billy but tragically perished in a car crash along with his dad.

Joanne Rossi (Allison McKenzie) 2002–2007

Phew, where do we start? Complicit in the murder of Marcus, had an affair – and baby – with her 'brother'. Jailed for pushing her mum down the stairs – even though it was her sister!

Joanne Rossi (Lisa Gardner) 2008–2011

Every bit as nasty as that other Jo, and had just as many men. Left (again) with handsome Leo after his brother Gabe decided she was just too nasty for him, and he was nasty!

Luca Rossi (Juan Pablo di Pace) 2005–2007

Met step-mum Gina while she was on holiday in Italy and returned with her. But he wasn't Franco's son so he celebrated by sleeping with Franco's daughter and fathering little Romeo. Been in: *Mamma Mia*.

Ruth Rossi (Morag Calder) 2002–2010

Lived in the shadow of Jo till the psychotic episodes took over. Wed Marty and Andy (though not at the same time), had a baby taken off her and left on a train with Scott.

Terry Samuels (Eric Robertson) 2012

Broke into the surgery for Lenny and acted all smug when approached by the police. Laughing on the other side of his face when they found a gun in his car.

Alisha Shah (Meneka Das) 2005–2006

Resident doc who fell in love with Cormac. Was already engaged to Zak and saved Cormac's bacon by dumping him! Then fell for Luca before going to live in India.

Arun Shah (Ricky Dhillon) 2005

Alisha's annoying brother briefly got together with Alanna to help launch her ill-fated modelling career before moving to London.

Dilip Shah (Aron Sidhu) 2005–2006

Second wave of the fractured Shah family. Wooed Nicki then worked as a delivery driver for Lenny – although Nicki wasn't impressed with what he was delivering.

Dr Vinnie Shah (Archie Lal) 2003–2004

Bubbly doctor loved a dose of his own medicine. Tried to snare Shazia and Eileen but the former fancied Heather and the latter, well, she fancied just about everyone else.

Annie Sobacz (Reanne Farley) 2010–

Roisin's cousin docked in Shieldinch with more secrets than an ancient gentlemen's organisation and quickly hooked up with Charlie. Been in: *The Ship*.

Callum Stuart (Donald Pirie) 2004–2005

Love interest of crazy Steph, evil Dr Marcus's daughter. Ended up as the twenty-seventh lover of Eileen (that year) and left for Edinburgh when he was accused of stealing money from the Deli.

Dr Miriam Stubbs (Kate Rutter) 2012–

There's a new partner in town, but one who decided to check out the practice by pretending to be a patient and discovered chaos as the fractured Brodie brood disintegrated in front of her!

Gordon Swan (Sandy Welch) 2009–2010

Salon owner and Hayley's secret dad. Fuming when Jack started going out with his daughter. Dated Ruth but Iona thought he was too boring for her!

Cammy Tennant (Neil Leiper) 2011–2012

The lowest of the low, predator Cammy did his best to get Stevie back on heroin – and succeeded. Surpassed himself by kidnapping Nicole to 'sell' her . . . till daddy Michael caught up with him.

Vader (Ryan Fletcher) 2004–2006

Initially a gang member who played his 'part' in the unforgettable Hazel–Vader–Alanna love triangle. Slept rough on Glasgow's mean streets after running away.

Reverend John Wallace (Jimmy Yuill) 2006, 2009

Looked after Scott post-overdose – until he found out his son ('You're no son of mine!') preferred men. Tried to get Scott to stop being gay, but gave up and went back to the islands.

Margaret Wallace (Anne Kidd) 2009

Moved in with Scott when her husband died. He tried everything to please his mum but it proved an impossible task. She hilariously thought Raymond was Scott's partner.

Scott Wallace (Tony Kearney) 2002–2010

Graphic designer who regularly incurred Ruth's wrath! Went out with DCI Eddie Hunter, psychotic Stevie Adams and Dan the Undertaker. Left on a train with Ruth. Never learn. Been in: *Machair*.

J.P. Walsh (Gary McCormack) 2003–2004

Tough guy J.P. was an old flame of Roisin. Bullied Raymond and Roisin shot him by mistake but he survived, until McCabe told his boys to 'take him away'.

DCI Richard Whiteside (Michael Nardone) 2007–2008

The nastiest copper on the planet. Eventually rumbled for his part in the murder of colleague DCI Hunter – even though the dogs in the street knew Lenny was responsible.

Johnny Wu (Richard Woo) 2007

Ran Wok My World until a gambling habit made him a prime takeover target for Lenny.

Susie Wu (Teo-Wa Vuong) 2007

Daughter of Johnny, Susie did everything to help him get free from debt but failed and worked as an escort while running Versus in Heather's absence.

Zak (Zak Hanif) 2005

Alisha's fiancé who turned up to spoil her cosy trysts with Cormac . . . after prompting from her brother Arun.

ACKNOWLEDGEMENTS

It's difficult to write a book like this without the help of a great many people. It was a genuine labour of love but would not have been possible without the help of the following:

Philip Barratt, Mark DiMeo, Jean Kerr, Ron Seeth, Stephen O'Donnell, Mark Dorris, Vikki Tennant, Ken McQuarrie, Stephen Greenhorn, Pat Campbell, Andy Drummond, Sinclair Gracie, Jamie McWilliam, Claire Pettifer, Helen McEwan, Daniel Wilson, Jim Shields, Martin Brocklebank, Graeme Gordon, Neil Mac, Anne O'Neill, Brian Gallagher, Susan Tauro, Annie Paterson, Julie Broadfoot, Jackie McGhee, Graeme Miller, Karen Higgins, Catherine Grieves, Frances Arnold, Morag Bain, and my family, my wife Elaine, kids Derek and Carey, and grandson Josh.

And a special thanks to Campbell, Kristen and the wonderful team at Black & White Publishing.

Pictures: Stephen Hughes, Mark Dorris, Ron Seeth, Jean Kerr, Mark DiMeo, Philip Barratt, Des O'Hare, Andy Drummond, Neil Mac, Iain G. Farrell, Alan Wylie, Pamela Byrne, Pete Oso Snell, Rosie Foley, Jeff Holmes.

And last, but by no means least . . . Johnny Beattie, Deirdre Davis, Pamela Byrne, Garry Sweeney, Stephen Purdon, Sally Howitt, Paul Samson, Eileen McCallum, Ryan Fletcher, Lisa Gardner, Paul James Corrigan, Keira Lucchesi, Tom Urie, Jacqueline Leonard, Lorna Anderson, Frank Gallagher, Billy McElhaney, Jenny Ryan, Libby McArthur, Tam Dean Burn, Jayd Johnson, Jason Pitt, Katie McEwan, Joyce Falconer, Lorraine McIntosh, Carter Ferguson, Barbara Rafferty, Claire Knight, Frances Healy, Holly Jack, Sarah McCardie, Sam Heughan, Carmen Pieraccini, Simon Weir and Neil Leiper.